CONFIRMATION

Spreading and Defending the Faith

John Sondag

IMAGE OF GOD SERIES

Educational and Theological Advisors

Rev. Richard M. Hogan / Rev. John M. LeVoir / Mary Jo Smith

Nihil Obstat: Frederick F. Campbell
Censor Librorum

Imprimatur: ✠ John R. Roach, D.D.
Archbishop of St. Paul and Minneapolis
April 13, 1993

Cover art: The Crosiers, Gene Plaisted, O.S.C.

For additional information about the Image of God program, call 1-800-635-3827.

Published 1993 by Ignatius Press, San Francisco

ISBN 0–89870–439–1
Printed in Hong Kong

Photo credits
1, 62: The Crosiers, Gene Plaisted, O.S.C. (Holy Spirit Church, St. Paul, Minn.).
3, 69: The Crosiers, Gene Plaisted, O.S.C. (Bishop Joseph Charron; St. Helena Church, Minneapolis, Minn.).
6: The Crosiers, Gene Plaisted, O.S.C. (St. Helena Church, Minneapolis, Minn.).
9: The Crosiers, Conrad Pickel (Christ the King Church, Minneapolis, Minn.).
10: The Crosiers, Gene Plaisted, O.S.C. (St. Gregory Church, Chicago, Il.).
13: The Crosiers, Gene Plaisted, O.S.C.
15: The Crosiers, Gene Plaisted, O.S.C.
16: The Crosiers, Gene Plaisted, O.S.C.
17: The Crosiers, Gene Plaisted, O.S.C.
18: The Crosiers, Gene Plaisted, O.S.C.
20 (left and right): James L. Shaffer.
23: The Crosiers, Gene Plaisted, O.S.C. (St. Joseph Church, Hammond, Ind.).
32: Leaflet Missal Company, St. Paul, Minn.
33: The Crosiers, Gene Plaisted, O.S.C. (Sacred Heart Church, Winona, Minn.).
36: The Crosiers, Gene Plaisted, O.S.C. (Lincoln Cathedral, England).
38: The Crosiers, Gene Plaisted, O.S.C. (Cardinal Glennon College, St. Louis, Mo.).
39: The Crosiers, Gene Plaisted, O.S.C. (Holy Spirit Church, St. Paul, Minn.).
40: Leaflet Missal Company, St. Paul, Minn.
42: The Crosiers, Gene Plaisted, O.S.C. (St. Joseph Cathedral, LaCrosse, Wisc.).
47: The Crosiers, Gene Plaisted, O.S.C. (Beverley Cathedral, England).
50: The Crosiers, Gene Plaisted, O.S.C. (St. Bernard Church, Madison, Wisc.).
51: The Crosiers, Gene Plaisted, O.S.C.
52: The Crosiers, Gene Plaisted, O.S.C. (St. Helena Church, Minneapolis, Minn.).
53: The Crosiers, Gene Plaisted, O.S.C. (St. John Church, Little Canada, Minn.).
54: Chico Anderson, Diocese of Duluth. Courtesy of the Visitation Sisters.
59: The Crosiers, Gene Plaisted, O.S.C. (St. Peter Church, Fallbrook, Calif.).
60: The Crosiers, Gene Plaisted, O.S.C.
61 (right and left): The Crosiers, Gene Plaisted, O.S.C.
65: Rev. Richard M. Hogan.
66: The Crosiers, Gene Plaisted, O.S.C. (Holy Spirit Church, St. Paul, Minn.).

CONTENTS

INTRODUCTION

Who? What? When? Where? Why? and How? are the standard questions a good journalist uses when writing a news article.

The "lead", or beginning, paragraph usually answers these questions. The answers capsulize the article and give readers essential information about a particular event. The remainder of the article expands upon the information found in the lead paragraph.

The standard news article is set up in an inverted pyramid form, in which the most important information is presented first and the least important last. This form enables a copy editor to cut out the last part of an article, if the newspaper does not have enough space for the entire article, and the reader can still obtain the essential information from the abbreviated article.

This textbook on Confirmation has a number of articles about Christ and His Church written in a newspaper format. You will be asked to analyze these articles and answer the essential questions—*Who? What? When? Where? Why?* and *How?*—so that you can capsulize important information about your Faith. By asking the journalist's six questions, you can arrive at essential elements of the Faith. The answers you uncover will assist you in understanding better the truths revealed to us by Christ and His Apostles. The better you understand your Faith, the better you will be able to live it and explain it to others.

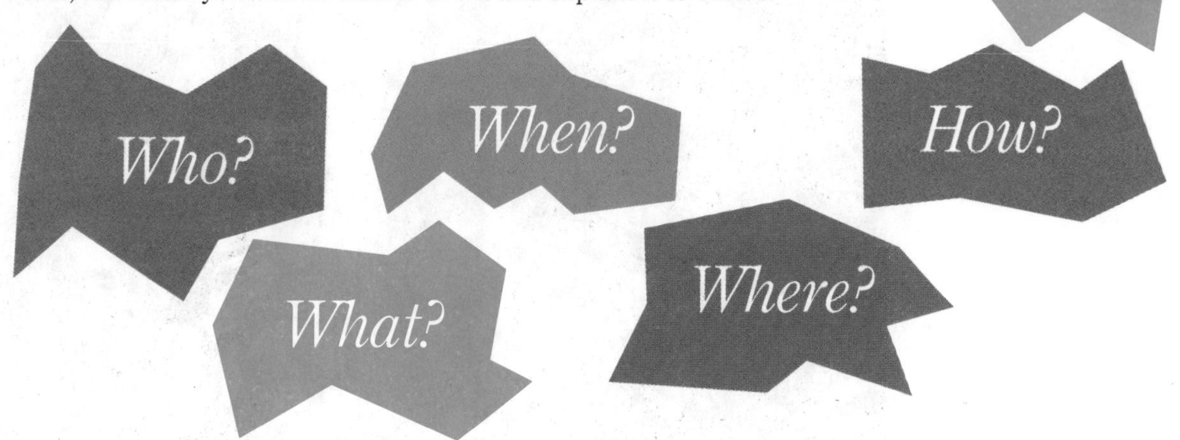

1 THE EARLY CHURCH

3,000 Jews Become Followers of the Late Jesus of Nazareth

JERUSALEM – Three thousand Jews were baptized in Jerusalem yesterday, becoming followers of the late Jesus of Nazareth after a series of unnatural events occurred on the Jewish feast of Pentecost. Jesus of Nazareth, who, having been crucified on Golgotha, died about 53 days before this feast, has been reported to have risen from the dead.

A group of followers of this former religious leader are led by a man named Peter. This band of followers had been praying in the upper room where Jesus had his last supper before his death. According to a follower of Jesus, named Luke, these disciples, including the mother of Jesus, had been gathered in prayer in this upper room for the previous nine days.

Bizarre events began to happen on the tenth day, which coincided with the Jewish feast of Pentecost. Luke said, "And suddenly there came from the sky a noise like a strong driving wind, and it filled the entire house in which they were.

"Then there appeared to them tongues as of fire, which parted and came to rest on each one of them", Luke continued. "And they were all filled with the Holy Spirit and began to speak in different tongues, as the Spirit enabled them to proclaim."

According to eyewitnesses, many Jews from outside Israel were in Jerusalem and assembled together as they all heard these followers speak in their own languages. The foreigners were able to understand these followers of Jesus as the disciples proclaimed their God's marvelous deeds.

Some persons in the crowd thought that the disciples of Jesus had been drinking too much. Peter, the leader of these followers, addressed the assembled and said, "These people are not drunk, as you suppose, for it is only nine o'clock in the morning."

Peter continued with a long speech about what had happened to their leader, Jesus, who had died. He told them that Jesus "was a man commended to you by God with mighty deeds, wonders, and signs, which God worked through him in your midst, as you yourselves know."

Jesus had been crucified and had risen from the dead, according to Peter. "Exalted at the right hand of God, he received the promise of the Holy Spirit from the Father and poured it forth, as you [both] see and hear."

After Peter boldly asserted that Jesus was "both Lord and Messiah", the assembled crowd was deeply moved and asked Peter and the other apostles, "What are we to do, my brothers?"

Peter answered, "Repent and be baptized, every one of you, in the name of Jesus Christ for the forgiveness of your sins; and you will receive the gift of the Holy Spirit."

According to Luke, approximately 3,000 persons were baptized after more testimony was presented to the crowd by Peter (Acts 2).

Mary, the Mother of Jesus of Nazareth, Stays with Disciples during Pentecost Event

JERUSALEM – Mary, the mother of Jesus of Nazareth, the man who died and who many have claimed has risen from the dead, was with the followers of Jesus during the recent Pentecost event. She was also with her son when he was crucified at Golgotha about two months ago.

In an interview, Mary was asked about the extraordinary series of events surrounding Pentecost. She said that her role was to be with her son's followers, because he had set up a structure for continuing to be present to the world.

Mary viewed her role as praying to her son, whom she said continues to live. She had stood beneath the cross as her son died, and she helped to lay his body in the tomb.

The mother of Jesus commented on how painful it had been for her to see her only child die such a cruel death, when she knew that he was an innocent man. "I knew I was helpless", she said, "but I also knew that he was doing the will of his Father in Heaven. I offered Him to His Father as He Himself poured out His life to His Father."

She related that she had found great joy in her son's rising from the dead, but that she missed him very much since he ascended into Heaven. "I long for the day when I can be with him and see him face to face.

"I know he is very much with me and that I can receive him at the Eucharistic Sacrifice that we celebrate", she continued, "but I still wait for the time when I can see him again."

Mary said that she plans to remain close to the followers of Jesus. One of them, by the name of John, has been said to be the appointed protector of Mary.

"I know that I can aid them in their work of bringing other people to believe in my son, Jesus", Mary commented. "Their work is a spiritual work, and I can be of service to them by praying to my son to assist them.

"I love my son, Jesus, and he loves me", she stated. "If I make a request to him, he is bound to grant it, if it is his Heavenly Father's will."

"I offered Him to His Father as He Himself poured out His life to His Father."

Peter, John Confirm in Samaria; Rebuke the Magician Simon

SAMARIA – Peter and John, two Apostles of the late Jesus of Nazareth, traveled from Jerusalem, to visit some of Jesus' followers. These disciples had already heard the word of God preached to them by Philip, and they had "been baptized", but they had not received the gift of the Holy Spirit through the imposition of hands (Confirmation).

Simon, a magician, wanted to buy the power of the Holy Spirit from the Apostles. "Give me this power too", Simon requested, "so that anyone upon whom I lay my hands may receive the Holy Spirit."

"May your money perish with you, because you thought that you could buy the gift of God with money", Peter responded. "Repent of this wickedness of yours and pray to the Lord that, if possible, your intention may be forgiven. For I see that you are filled with bitter gall and are in the bonds of iniquity."

The magician replied, "Pray for me to the Lord, that nothing of what you have said may come upon me" (Acts 8).

Council Clarifies Teaching on Salvation

JERUSALEM – The first Church Council held in Jerusalem decided yesterday to permit Gentiles (non-Jews) to be received into the body of believers without first being circumcised. The first group of followers of Jesus of Nazareth had been Jews, while some of the recent converts to the new religion have been Gentiles.

After considerable discussion, Peter, the head of the Apostles, spoke at the assembly, saying, "We believe that we are saved through the grace of the Lord Jesus, in the same way as they [the Gentiles]". Much discussion among the Apostles and presbyters ensued after a delegation from Antioch told about the conversion of Gentiles to the Faith.

Led by Paul and Barnabas, this delegation came to Jerusalem after dissension had arisen in Antioch because a group of followers of Jesus insisted that Gentiles should be circumcised when they became part of this new religion. The delegation came to the Church authorities in Jerusalem to settle the dispute. Followers of Jesus believe that the Holy Spirit guides a Council so that the Apostles would correctly interpret the will of Christ.

The same Council further decided that converts from the Gentiles would not have to observe other Jewish practices except "to abstain from meat sacrificed to idols, from blood, from meats of strangled animals, and from unlawful marriage." The Council sent two representatives, Judas Barsabbas and Silas, to the Church in Antioch to deliver a letter from the Council about the decisions of the assembly (Acts 15).

Pope Paul VI Issues New Document to Update Sacrament of Confirmation

ROME – Yesterday, on August 15, 1971, Pope Paul VI issued a letter here addressed to the entire Catholic Church on the sacrament of Confirmation to update the liturgical celebration of that sacrament and to assist the faithful in understanding better the effects that this sacrament has on the lives of Catholics.

The letter, entitled *Apostolic Constitution on the Sacrament of Confirmation*, not only explains the sacrament of Confirmation, it also shows that sacrament's relationship to the other sacraments of initiation: Baptism and Eucharist. All three sacraments are related, and together they initiate a person into the life of Christ and His Church.

Pope Paul VI explained in the document that the spiritual life has a certain likeness to the natural life. "The sharing in the divine nature which is granted to all people through the grace of Christ has a certain likeness to the origin, development, and nourishing of natural life", he wrote.

"The faithful are born anew by baptism, strengthened by the sacrament of confirmation, and finally are sustained by the food of eternal life in the eucharist", the Pope continued. The document further explained the effects of each of these three sacraments.

"In baptism, the newly baptized receive forgiveness of sins, adoption as sons of God, and the character of Christ, by which they are members of the Church and for the first time become sharers in the priesthood of their Savior", Pope Paul VI stated.

The sacrament of Confirmation confers a special outpouring of the Holy Spirit, Who gives "special strength". "Moreover, having received the character of this sacrament, they are 'bound more intimately to the Church' and 'they are more strictly obliged to spread and defend the faith both by word and by deed as true witnesses of Christ' ", the Pope continued.

Pope Paul VI also explained that the sacrament of Confirmation should be administered in the following manner. It is to be "conferred through the anointing with Chrism on the forehead, which is done by the laying on of the hand, and through the words: 'Be sealed with the Gift of the Holy Spirit.' "

Baptism—Related to Confirmation

To understand the sacrament of Confirmation, it is necessary to understand the sacrament of Baptism. Exactly what does the sacrament of Baptism do for the person receiving it?

The sacrament, which consists in the pouring of water with the words "I baptize you in the name of the Father and of the Son and of the Holy Spirit", has several effects. Baptism first of all cleanses an individual of all sin, both original sin and any actual sins that might have been committed. This enables the baptized person to be a friend of the Lord, something that would have been impossible if the person had not been freed from original sin or any mortal sin. For original sin deprived Adam and Eve and all their descendants of the sanctifying grace that made them friends with God.

Through Baptism, which forgives sins, you are made a friend of God. Baptism, through the power of the Holy Spirit, unites you to Jesus, Who becomes your Brother. You, then, become an adopted child of the Father.

Through this union with Jesus, you take on the character of Christ. Because Christ and His Church are one, you, then, become united with the Church and enter and become a member of the Church.

The baptized person also becomes a sharer in the priesthood of Jesus, Who offers Himself to His Heavenly Father, particularly in the sacrifice of the Mass. You, therefore, are given the responsibility of offering praise and worship to the Heavenly Father through words and deeds.

The baptized person is not only made a priest (not an ordained priest), but also a prophet and a king. For Jesus is Priest, Prophet, and King. As a prophet, you have the responsibility of bringing the Good News of salvation to others. As a king, you serve, and you have dominion over the created world by reordering all things according to Christ's will.

Because Baptism has made you an adopted child of the Father, it also has made you an heir to heaven. You now can attain heaven for all eternity, so long as you do not forfeit heaven by dying in the state of mortal sin.

Baptism also gives you the gifts of faith, hope, and charity, which enable the baptized person to know God, to hope in Him, and to love Him and His other sons and daughters. This first sacrament of initiation also confers the seven gifts of the Holy Spirit: wisdom, understanding, knowledge, counsel, fortitude, piety, and fear of the Lord.

Baptism, then, is the first sacrament all Catholics must receive before any of the other sacraments. It is the sacrament that applies to each person the merits of Jesus' death and Resurrection, which won salvation for all mankind.

Through the power of the Holy Spirit, then, Baptism is given as a means of personal salvation. The individual is redeemed and born into the life of God. This initial life is further strengthened and nourished by the work of the Holy Spirit in the sacraments of Confirmation and Holy Eucharist.

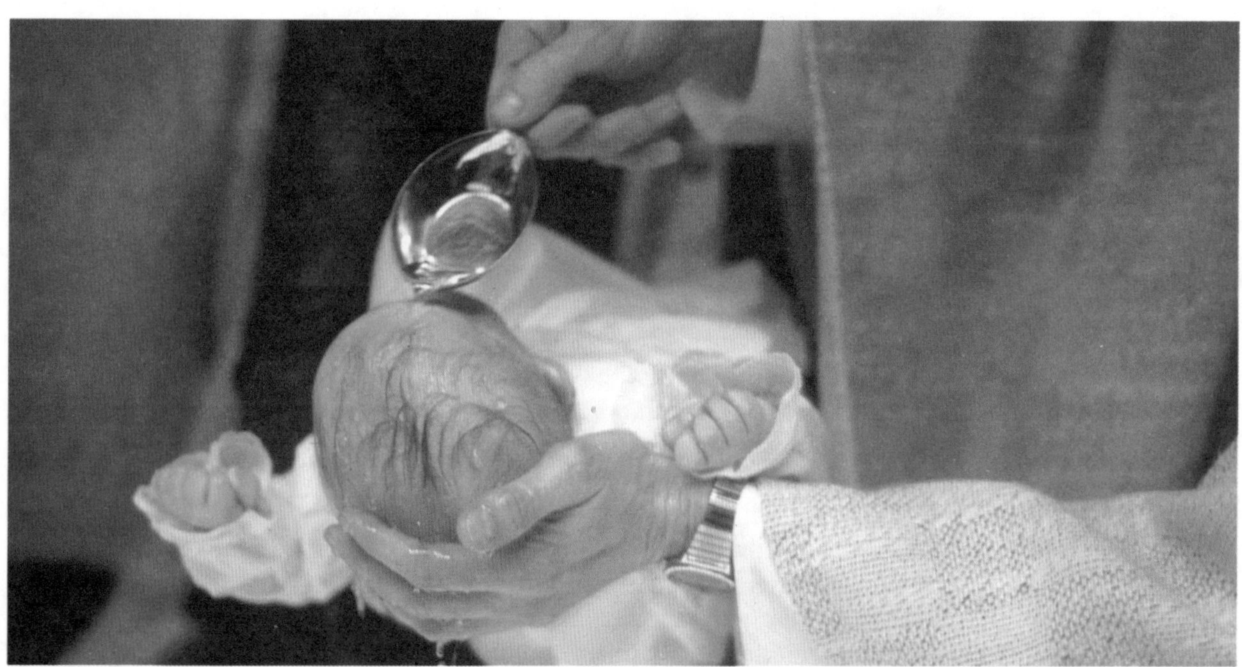

Effects of the sacrament of Baptism

1. Takes away all sin (original and actual), which deprives one of friendship with God.
2. Gives sanctifying grace, which establishes a friendship with God.
3. Makes us adopted children of God.
4. Confers the character of Christ.
5. Makes us members of Christ's Church.
6. Makes us priests, prophets, and kings.
7. Confers the three theological virtues of faith, hope, and charity.
8. Bestows the seven gifts of the Holy Spirit.
9. Makes us heirs of heaven.
10. Applies the merits of Jesus' death and Resurrection.

Confirmation—What Is It?

The sacrament of Confirmation is a special outpouring of the Holy Spirit in which a baptized person is sealed with the gift of the Third Person of the Blessed Trinity. Granted, the baptized person has already received the Holy Spirit in Baptism, but this special sealing with the Holy Spirit is given to bind the person even more closely to Christ and His Church.

Baptism is given for personal salvation, but Confirmation is given to thrust an individual outward and send that person on a "mission". Confirmation is the Pentecost event for a baptized person. Like the disciples who received the Holy Spirit at Pentecost and went out to proclaim the Good News about Jesus Christ, those who are confirmed are given the Holy Spirit to energize them "to spread and defend the Catholic Faith both by word and by deed as true witnesses of Christ" (*Apostolic Constitution on the Sacrament of Confirmation*).

The gift of the Holy Spirit in Confirmation is given to bind you more closely to Christ and His Church, and the mission of the Church is to bring others to Christ by speech and action. The purpose of Confirmation is to help you fulfill your responsibilities within the mission of the Church. Through the sacrament of Confirmation, you are given the grace to become an active agent for Christ, and not merely a passive recipient of God's gifts.

In the sacrament of Baptism you have been anointed priest, prophet, and king, in order to give worship to God, to proclaim the Good News, and to serve others and reorder creation according to Christ's will. In Confirmation, these responsibilities are energized by the Holy Spirit, so that you, as a member of the Church, will take on the tasks connected with these offices of Jesus Christ, which have now been delegated by Him to the Church.

Confirmation strengthens the gifts of faith, hope, and charity and the seven gifts of the Holy Spirit, which were given for the first time in the sacrament of Baptism. Now, as these gifts are strengthened, they can be used to spread and defend the Faith.

As a defender of the Faith, you are made a soldier of Christ, that is, someone willing to withstand attacks against the Catholic Faith, even to the point of death. You are a soldier of Christ in a spiritual sense, not in the sense of being willing to face physical battles. But a soldier of Christ might well be asked to suffer persecution for the sake of the Catholic Faith, and you will have the spiritual strengthen to defend the Faith when it comes under attack from others.

To show the connection between Confirmation and Pentecost, the normal minister of Confirmation is a bishop, because the bishops are successors of the Apostles, who were present at the first Pentecost. In special situations, the bishop may delegate a priest to administer the sacrament of Confirmation.

Finding Meaning in One's Life because of the Sacrament of Confirmation

"You will be sent!" "You will have a mission!"

That mission was given to you when you were baptized, but that mission will be strengthened and energized when you receive the sacrament of Confirmation. For that sacrament will bestow on you a special outpouring of the Holy Spirit to send you into the world "to spread and defend the Catholic Faith both by word and deed as true witnesses of Christ".

Because you are sent by the Holy Spirit to spread and defend the Faith, you will always have a purpose in life. This means that you will have to look for opportunities to bring the Good News of salvation to the people around you.

These opportunities are plentiful, because all people can grow in their understanding and love of Jesus. Every day you will be with people (relatives, friends, neighbors, teachers, and people with whom you work) who need to hear and see that the redemption affects their lives.

We can spread the Good News by talking to others about the Faith and also by our example, that is, our good deeds of service to others. If you look for opportunities to spread the Good News, you will find them everywhere.

You do not have to talk about Jesus all the time to give witness to your Faith. You can show others that you are a believer by living your Faith and by doing acts of service and kindness.

Even someone sick in bed or dying of cancer has the opportunity and the mission to bring others to Christ by word and deed. Of course, one effective way to bring others to the Lord is by prayer, and ill or disabled persons can lovingly offer their pain and suffering to the Father with the sacrificial death of Jesus on the Cross for sinners, for the missions, for the good of the Church, or for others who need prayers.

St. Thérèse of Lisieux, of the Child Jesus, is the patroness of missions in the Church. She was a young nun who died at the age of 24, who never went to the foreign missions herself. She did, however, offer her prayers and actions for those in need, particularly those in the missions, so she was proclaimed a patroness of missions.

Someone who constantly looks for ways to spread the Faith will find ways, because opportunities exist all around us. Each morning a baptized and confirmed person has a good reason to get up—the mission to spread the Good News to others!

Father John Maronic, O.M.I., Founds Victim Missionary Group for Sick and Disabled Persons

BELLEVILLE, ILLINOIS – Fr. John Maronic, O.M.I., founded a group to help chronically ill and disabled people see their suffering in the light of the Gospel. This group, called the Victim Missionaries, has as its goal assisting its members to unite their sufferings with the sacrifice of Jesus' death on the Cross.

Fr. Maronic, who has been working at the National Shrine of Our Lady of the Snows, gathered a group of handicapped and sick persons together in order to support one another in a Christian understanding of their suffering. Because the sick and disabled were traveling to Marian Shrines throughout the world, Fr. Maronic decided to organize them as they came to the National Shrine of Our Lady of the Snows.

A member of the religious order called the Missionary Oblate of Mary Immaculate, Fr. Maronic called this new organization "Victim Missionaries" because he wanted the sick and disabled to understand that they could offer their sufferings to their Heavenly Father in imitation of Jesus, an innocent Victim, Who gave His life for all sinners. He used the word "missionaries" because he hoped that the members of this group would see themselves as missionaries sent to help the Church by offering their prayers and sufferings for the good of the Church.

Fr. Maronic saw the sick and the disabled as a real "gold mine", ready to be tapped for the good of the Church. "This suffering will be wasted if we do not help these people see that their lives can bear spiritual fruit for the rest of the Church", he said.

Members of the Victim Missionaries gather together once a month for a day of recollection, in which they have conferences on the spiritual life, pray together, and celebrate the Sacrifice of the Mass.

Confirmation Is Linked to the Sacrament of the Eucharist

Baptism, Confirmation, and Holy Eucharist are related to one another, and together they are called the sacraments of initiation, because they initiate and draw those who receive them more deeply into the life of Christ and His Church.

The Holy Eucharist is the sacrament that perfectly expresses our relationship with Christ and His Church. When we receive this great sacrament, we are united with Jesus Himself as He is risen from the dead. When we receive the Eucharist, we receive the Risen Lord.

When we receive the Eucharist, we are also united with the rest of the Church, for, in the Eucharist, members of the Church become one in the Lord, just as grains of wheat come together to form one bread. The Eucharist perfectly expresses the Church coming together and being united to Jesus.

Those who have been baptized and confirmed are sent as priests, prophets, and kings to serve Jesus and His Church. As missionaries and ambassadors of Jesus and His Church, they are to draw all people together in faith, hope, and charity, so that they will be able to give praise and honor to the Father.

We were created to know and love the Lord, and Baptism and Confirmation help us to know and love the Lord. In the Eucharist we have the perfect opportunity to know Jesus and to give ourselves totally to Jesus, Who, in union with the Holy Spirit, presents us to His Father.

We can offer our studies to the Lord as a prayer of praise to our heavenly Father . . .

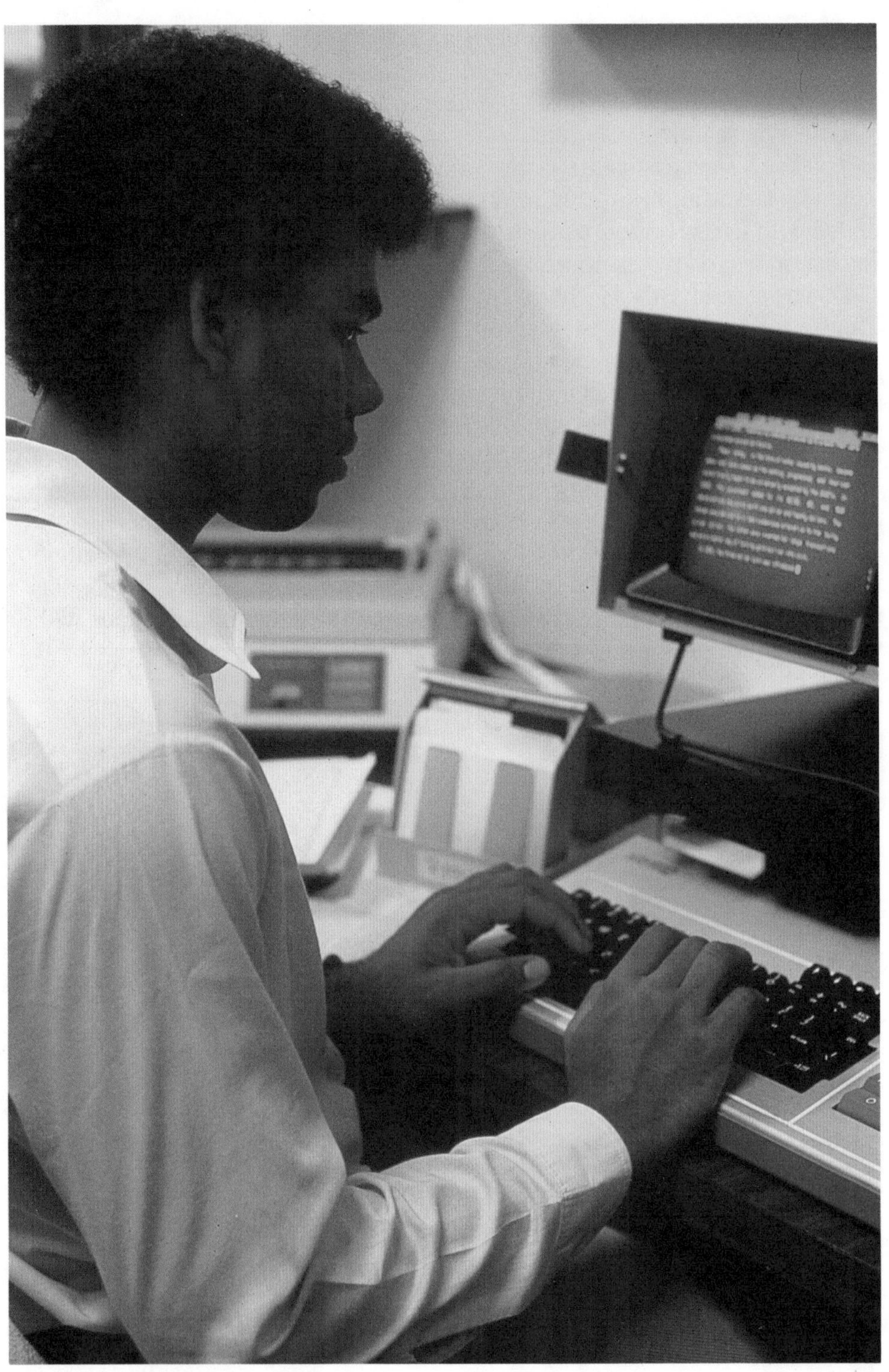

3 THE MYSTICAL PERSON—CHRIST AND THE CHURCH

By our Baptism, we became united to Jesus Christ, and we were united to the other members of His Church. Christ and all the members of the Church form one mystical person. As Pope John Paul II quotes from St. Augustine, "Christ and the Church are one single mystical person."

That means that you have a role to perform in the Church. The Church has many members, and we all have a role to play in its activity.

All of us need to figure out what role we play in the Church. Just as each person in a family must cooperate with the other members of the family, so too, as members of the Church, we cooperate with Christ and others in the Church.

At this point in our lives we are called to be students, so it is important to study well in preparation for adult roles in the Church. The more prepared we become through our studies, the better we will be able to serve the Church in the future.

We can offer our studies to the Lord as a prayer of praise to our Heavenly Father and as a prayer of petition for sinners, missionaries, or others who need our prayers. Our desk can become an altar on which we offer our sacrifices to the Lord. These sacrifices can, then, be presented to the Lord every time we participate in the Sacrifice of the Mass.

But our lives have more aspects to them than study. We are sons, daughters, brothers, sisters, friends, or neighbors. We participate in sports, play musical instruments, or have hobbies. We read books, watch TV, and go to movies.

All these relationships and activities involve our virtues and talents. We are better children of our parents if we have the virtues of charity, respect, obedience, patience, and generosity. We are better friends if we are patient, understanding, and forgiving.

Some of us have athletic talent, while others have the ability to play musical instruments or to sing. Maybe some of us are good with computers, while others are good at cooking.

All these virtues and talents can be put at the service of the Lord and His Church, if we offer them to the Lord. Some can be directly put at the service of the Lord, for instance, by making a cake for a bake sale at church or by singing in a church choir. We should look for ways in which we can help our parish and our Catholic institutions, because they help to build up the mystical person of Christ through the sacramental, educational, or service functions that they provide.

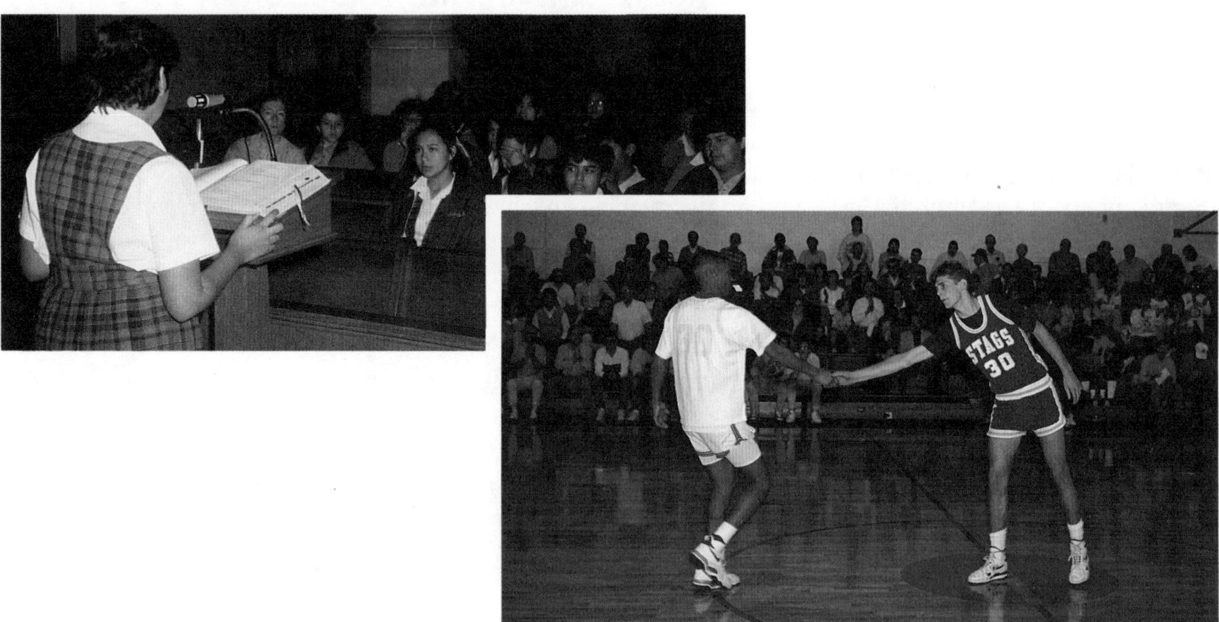

But it is not only in church-related activities that we can use our talents for building up the mystical person of Christ. We can offer a basketball or baseball game to the Lord as a prayer of worship and petition for sinners to come back to the Church or for some other need. We can start off the game with a prayer in our hearts like the following: "Jesus, thank You for the ability to play basketball. Help me to play well. I give this game (or practice session) to You as a gift of my love, and I offer it as a prayer for sinners who need my prayers."

The "Morning Offering" is another way of presenting our virtues and talents to the Lord, for in that prayer we offer "our prayers, works, joys, and sufferings" of each day to the Lord for special intentions of the Church. Even though we say this prayer at the beginning of each day, we can pause throughout the day and offer what we are doing to the Lord. It is a way of lovingly recognizing that our virtues and talents come from Him and should be returned to Him.

The celebration of Mass, however, is the best way of offering our lives to the Lord. For in the Mass we have the sacrifice of Jesus' death on the Cross made present. We have the chance to offer all our virtues and talents to the Father with Jesus, as He offers Himself to the Father in the same sacrifice He offered on the Cross.

We were not present for the Paschal Mystery, Jesus' dying on the Cross and rising from the dead, the most important and central event of all history. But God in His wisdom has made this event present to us every time Mass is celebrated. So, each time we go to Mass, it is as if we are standing beneath the Cross with Mary, offering Jesus to the Father and offering our own sacrifices, prayers, virtues, and talents to the Father through Jesus' sacrifice.

What Virtues and Talents Has God Given Me?

The Lord has given each person a variety of virtues and talents to serve Him. When each of us uses these gifts from the Lord, and we work together as one family, His Church, then Jesus' Heavenly Father is glorified.

To use these gifts well, it is important that we know what these virtues and talents are. Make a list of your talents, write ways in which they can be used in the Church, and be sure to thank God regularly for His gift of these talents.

When listing these virtues and talents, make sure to remember the three theological virtues of faith, hope, and charity, which were given to you in Baptism and which will be strengthened and deepened by the sacrament of Confirmation. In addition, remember to list the seven gifts of the Holy Spirit, also given in Baptism and strengthened and deepened in Confirmation.

Virtue or Talent	How It Can Be Used to Serve . . .		
	God	**The Church**	**Others**
Faith	Praise of God	Praying for sinners, vocations, and so forth	Praying for peace
Hope	Having confidence that God gives grace when we do good for others	Encouraging others in Church to trust God when they are suffering	Helping others see that God will help them in their difficulties
Charity	Celebrating the Eucharist, where I become one with Christ and the Church	Helping with a parish festival	Shoveling snow or running errands for an elderly person
Mathematics	Offering classes or homework to God as an act of love	Offering classes or homework as a prayer for missionaries	Tutoring a younger student who is having trouble in math classes
Singing	Singing in the parish choir	Christmas caroling with other parishioners	Being in a school musical
Athletics	Offering games or practice to God as an act of thanksgiving	Offering games or practice to God as prayer for the parish	Playing a benefit game to raise money for a charitable cause
Writing	Writing a story with spiritual values	Writing an article that informs others about a Church project	Writing an article that expresses Christian ethical values
Cooking	Offering cooking to God as an act of thanksgiving	Making some cakes or cookies for a bake sale	Bringing some cookies to a shut-in

The Parable of the Talents

Read Matthew 25:14–30. In this Scripture passage, we see three servants being given certain amounts of money (a talent at the time of Jesus was a measurement of money). Two of the servants use the money well, but one buried the talent. The master who gave these servants the money is pleased with the two who doubled his money but is upset with the one who buried the money.

In applying this passage to our lives, we ask ourselves if our Master, the Lord, has given us, His servants, some talents, not necessarily money, but virtues, such as faith, courage, and patience, and talents, such as a good mind, musical ability, or athletic skills. Our talents have been given to us to use well. In reflecting on this passage, ask yourself these questions:

Have you ever been afraid to use your talents? Fear can paralyze you when you would like to do good things.

What are some things that cause you to be afraid?

- Ridicule? Friends making fun of you?
- Making a mistake? Doing the wrong thing?
- Losing time or money and not receiving back what you have given up?
- Being embarrassed? Thinking someone won't like you?
- Being put out of the group? Being called names?

In thinking about how we are to use the talents God has given us, we may recall times when others have made fun of us. This can be painful, but many times persons who do great things for society must bear the brunt of a few people poking fun at them. Just think of all the cartoons in the newspapers making fun of the President of the United States. The President knows that some of his decisions may be unpopular. But should he not act because others may poke fun at him, the whole country might suffer.

If we are afraid that others will make fun of us when we make a speech in public or play the piano for elderly residents in a nursing home, then the people who could benefit from our good works may never receive the fruits of our labors. If we are afraid of being ridiculed for doing what is right—going to church on Sunday or staying sober when our friends get drunk—then others will not reap the reward of our prayer or friendship.

Some of us are just afraid of making mistakes, because we are perfectionists. We have to do things the very best we can or not do them at all. When there is a possibility of making a mistake, we become paralyzed and do not act. We won't sing in public, make a speech, or write a poem, because what we do may not be perfect. Others never benefit, then, from our good works.

We may think that serving others or giving of our talents and virtues demand too much time and energy on our part. We may be afraid that we will lose some of the free time we have for ourselves. What we forget, however, is that we have been made by God to be happy, and the way we attain happiness is to give ourselves entirely to what is truthful, good, and beautiful. Because God is

Then Jesus said to his disciples, "Whoever wishes to come after me must deny himself, take up his cross, and follow me. For whoever wishes to save his life will lose it, but whoever loses his life for my sake will find it. What profit would there be for one to gain the whole world and forfeit his life? Or what can one give in exchange for his life? For the Son of Man will come with his angels in his Father's glory, and then he will repay everyone according to his conduct. Amen, I say to you, there are some standing here who will not taste death until they see the Son of Man coming in his kingdom."

—Mt 16:24–28

pure Truth, Goodness, and Beauty, we will never be unhappy or lose out when we serve Him or others because we love Him.

As the bishops of Vatican Council II wrote: "Man can fully discover his true self only in a sincere giving of himself." Our talents are given to us by God so that we can use them to give ourselves in love to God and to our neighbor.

Leader of New Religious Group Explains the Social Dynamic of Christians

Paul the Apostle is a leading figure in the new religious group calling themselves "Christians". These followers of Jesus of Nazareth, whom they believe has risen from the grave after being put to death on a cross, have as their leaders men called "Apostles".

In a recent interview, Paul talked about the Church, or organization of Christians. In a letter to believers in the city of Corinth Paul had referred to the Christians as the "Body of Christ".

A human body expresses a person. Christ's body expressed His divine Person. Thus, if it is true that the Church is the body of Christ, Paul seems to be implying that it is in some mysterious way the person of Christ. This teaching affects the way Christians treat one another and the manner in which they use their gifts and talents.

Paul wrote in that same letter that "the body is not a single part, but many. If a foot should say, 'Because I am not a hand I do not belong to the body,' it does not for this reason belong any less to the body" (1 Cor 12:14–15).

Paul further explained that "God placed the parts, each one of them, in the body as he intended. If they were all one part, where would the body be?" (1 Cor 12:18–19).

The importance of each person in the Church was pointed out in Paul's letter when he said, "But God has so constructed the body as to give greater honor to a part that is without it, so that there may be no division in the body, but that the parts may have the same concern for one another" (1 Cor 12:24–25).

Paul explained that believers are joined together in the risen Jesus in a rite called the sacrament of Baptism. Because of this union in the Lord, they are also united to one another.

According to Paul, God has set up a priority of functions based on the gifts the Holy Spirit has given to the members of the Church. Apostles are first, then prophets, teachers, miracle workers, healers, assistants, administrators, and those who speak in tongues.

Paul pointed out that the greatest gift, which surpasses all the gifts given to the Church, is charity, namely, love of God and neighbor. This is a gift given to all the baptized believers, and it endures beyond death, when many of the other gifts given to the Church cease.

In his letter, Paul wrote that there are three great gifts from God: faith, hope and love; "but the greatest of these is love" (1 Cor 12:13).

How Do You Discern Your Vocation?

"Vocation" means a "call". To hear a call, one must listen. In order to hear what Jesus is asking you to do, you must listen. Jesus may be calling you in a variety of ways, so how should you listen to Jesus?

1. Pray.

Our prayers should include quiet time to listen to Jesus speak. We can do that by thinking about the Scriptures or other prayers we say. As we think about them and try to apply them to our lives, the Holy Spirit may inspire us through certain thoughts that strike our minds. Jesus sometimes uses these thoughts to speak to us. We should pray the words: "Speak, Lord, your servant is listening" and "Lord, show me what you want me to do, for I come to do your will."

2. Listen to the Church.

Learn and know what the Church teaches, because Jesus speaks to us today through the Church. We know that the Pope and the bishops are the official teachers who speak in the name of Jesus, so we should always match thoughts from our prayer with what the Church teaches. Sometimes our thoughts in prayer could be our own selfish desires, rather than Jesus teaching us, but if our thoughts go contrary to the Church's teaching, we will know they are not Jesus' words.

3. Talk to your pastors, parents, and teachers.

Ask these people who practice their Faith how they think you can best serve the Church with your specific talents. They can give you some indication as to whether you have the ability to pursue a certain vocation. If you want to be a priest or religious, your pastor, parents, or teachers can discuss with you whether you have the mental ability and physical health necessary. You should have the advice of several persons (parents, priests, and teachers), because each one sees you in different ways.

Special Callings within the Church

Jesus calls us to do special tasks within the Church. Just as a human body has certain parts that can function only in a certain manner, so too within the Church all have different roles to play.

Each person's responsibilities are important. The members of the Church meet their responsibilities by following the call of Christ.

You should not seek a role in the Church because of its power or prestige, but because Christ is calling you to this task or role. By following Christ's call, you are led to holiness. The Church has had Popes who are saints, and it has had young people whose roles were relatively insignificant also become saints. When you are faithful to Christ's calling, you can help others to become holy also.

■ Within the Church, some are called to the religious life, in which men or women take vows of poverty, chastity, and obedience. They take these vows to dedicate themselves more fully to Christ and to express their total love for Him. Those who take these vows are usually priests, sisters, or brothers in religious orders. Out of love for God, they promise Him that they will give up material possessions, they will not get married, and they will live in obedience to a religious superior.

■ Some men are called to be ordained. This vocation enables the Church to have the Gospel preached and the sacraments celebrated, particularly the Eucharist. Men who are called to be ordained participate in a special way in the priesthood of Jesus Christ. Bishops participate in the fullness of the priesthood of Jesus; priests and deacons also share in this priesthood of Christ through the sacrament of Holy Orders. Both bishops and priests are required to make a promise of celibacy, and deacons may make a promise of celibacy or they may be married, provided they are married before they are ordained. If a deacon's wife dies, he may not marry again.

■ Some men and women are called to the sacrament of marriage. This vocation enables a man and a woman by their marriage to become a sign of Christ's love for His Church. Together their enduring marital love represents the total union of Christ and His Church. God gives a husband and wife the grace to have a love for one another that is permanent, faithful, and open to new life.

■ Some men and women are called by God to the single life. By following God's will they are often given the opportunity to devote more time to God and neighbor. They can live a Christian life being a good example for others. Many single people are free to serve others through volunteer work or to serve the Church as lay missionaries.

4 THE HOLY SPIRIT AND TRUTH

Good journalists seek the truth. People become frustrated and irritated when they find out that newspapers have inaccuracies or distortions of the truth.

That people are upset with newspapers when they do not print the truth is understandable, because our minds seek the truth in order to know what is good. God made us so that we can know what is good and then love the good.

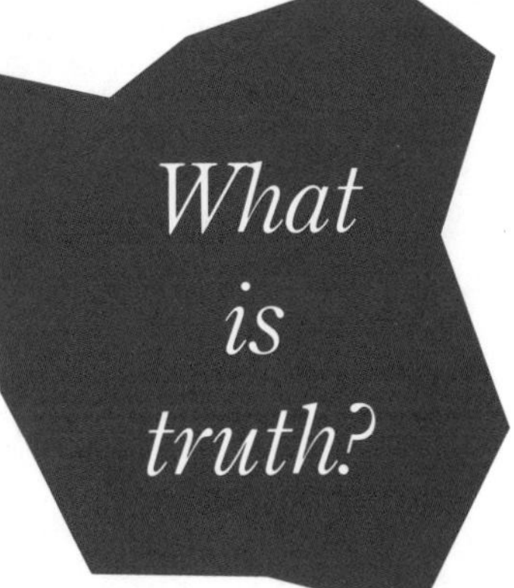

This is what it means to be made in the image and likeness of God, for we are made like God, Who knows and loves. Just as He has an intellect and a will, He gave us an intellect to know and a will to love.

Once we know what is right, we can choose to pursue what is right or make the right decision. For example, once a woman knows abortion is the destruction of a human life, she can choose not to have an abortion. She will love the baby in her womb, rather than destroying her child.

The responsibility of a Catholic who has received the sacrament of Confirmation is to spread and defend the Faith. This means that a confirmed person has the opportunity to participate more fully in the mission of Jesus and His Church by bringing the truths of God to others, so they can know God and love Him.

God not only gives us the truth to know but allows us to be a part of His mission to bring the truth to others by what we say and do. Many times, because we choose to do the right thing or do some good action ourselves, we are witnesses to the goodness of God. Many people take notice of the truths of the Catholic Faith because they have witnessed the goodness of those who believe in Jesus and His Church. That goodness moves the hearts of others to listen to the truth.

As baptized and confirmed Catholics, we need to be able to speak intelligently about the Faith and to live out the Faith, so that we can give witness to Christ and His Church. This chapter will present some newspaper accounts of people in the Church who have been good teachers of the Faith. They have spoken intelligently to others, and their lives are examples to us of how to bring the Good News of salvation to the people we meet.

ASSIGNMENT

Writing an Interview Article

Good reporters know how to interview persons who are knowledgeable about certain topics. Efficient reporters think about questions they can ask during an interview, and they frequently write them down on paper before the interview.

Good interviewers also try to think of questions during the interview itself. Some of the answers from the person being interviewed may provoke questions that were not formulated before the interview.

One way to learn how people bring the "Good News" of Jesus to others by their words is to interview them. Your assignment will be to interview three teachers of the Faith, that is, persons who spread the Gospel by what they say. These can be parents, pastors, sisters or brothers from religious orders, deacons, teachers, catechists, your sponsors, parishioners, neighbors, or friends who are able to explain well the Catholic Faith to other persons.

Write one long feature article about all three persons or write a short report on each interview. Remember to quote the persons accurately or to summarize their statements in as accurate a fashion as possible. The truth is extremely important.

Here are some questions you may want to ask:

What kind of work do you do? Do you have regular opportunities to talk with others about Jesus and His Church? Is it your responsibility to teach about the Faith?

Do you have opportunities to try consciously to teach others about Jesus Christ and His Church? What are some of these opportunities? Are they a part of your vocation? Do you look for opportunities to explain the Faith to others?

Are you ever criticized or ridiculed because of what you say or teach?

Do you ever think about how the gifts of the Holy Spirit, which have been strengthened in the sacrament of Confirmation, help you?

Do you rely on the sacraments to help you to be strong in your work or teaching? Do you ever pray that the Holy Spirit will help you to teach others about Jesus and His Church? Do you have a conscious appreciation of how prayer and the sacraments help you to teach the Faith to others?

Do you continue to read or go to classes to deepen your understanding about the Faith? Do you look to the Pope and the bishops as your guide in your teaching?

Can you remember feeling frustrated when you thought you were not teaching well? Are there times when you were satisfied that your teaching, with God's help, made a difference in others' lives?

Four Gifts of the Holy Spirit: Wisdom, Understanding, Counsel, and Knowledge

When God extends His hand of friendship in the sacrament of Baptism, He lavishly bestows many gifts. Besides the three theological virtues of faith, hope, and charity, He also grants the seven gifts of the Holy Spirit, namely, wisdom, understanding, counsel, knowledge, fortitude, piety, and fear of the Lord.

Wisdom, understanding, counsel, and knowledge help us to know God better and to know how to love and serve Him in order to attain happiness with Him for all eternity. Because we were created in the image and likeness of God to know and love, these four gifts of the Holy Spirit assist our minds in being more like God.

Wisdom is the gift of the Holy Spirit that helps us to respond to the things of God and assists us in evaluating everything we do in light of these things. Wisdom helps us to decide whether something we are doing is really worthwhile in relation to our goal of being with God for all eternity. Wisdom also helps us to think about the teachings of the Faith and how these teachings help us to judge all things according to the Faith.

Understanding helps our minds to grasp the truths of our Faith in a simple yet profound manner. This gift assists us to find meaning in what we believe.

Counsel helps our minds to know what is right in specific situations. It also helps us to know how to help others by our words and actions. The Holy Spirit advises us in our actions.

Knowledge helps to judge all things in relation to God. For instance, this gift will help us to have sorrow for our sins and failures, because we see what we have done in relation to God. Knowledge will also help us to see that all created things have little meaning except in the light of eternity.

These four gifts are given in Baptism to help us to follow Christ and to grow in holiness. They are given for our salvation.

In the sacrament of Confirmation, these gifts of wisdom, understanding, counsel, and knowledge are strengthened, not only for our salvation, but primarily to help us to spread and defend the Faith in what we say and do. These gifts of the Holy Spirit enlighten the mind and help us to say the right things in explaining the Faith to others. They will also enable us to know how we should act as witnesses to the Faith.

Our Lord is the One Who wants to draw all people to Himself. It is His grace and assistance that will help us bring others to Him. In the sacrament of Confirmation the gifts of the Holy Spirit are energized in a special fashion in order to assist us in our mission of drawing others to Christ and His Church.

. . . he leaves "no stone unturned" in bringing Jesus' teachings to the world

Pope John Paul II

A Modern Teacher

Pope John Paul II is a teacher of the Faith. To get his message to as many people as possible he uses many means—television, radio, newspapers, various writings, public and private audiences, meetings and rallies.

To communicate Christ's message of salvation the Pope travels thousands of miles each year to visit young and old; healthy, infirm, and disabled people; the rich and the poor. When he visits a foreign country to teach, he tries to learn and use their language so that he can communicate effectively with his audiences.

Pope John Paul II knows how important his message is, so he leaves "no stone unturned" in bringing Jesus' teachings to the world. He has seen the Catholic Faith lived in his homeland, Poland, where Catholics suffered persecution from both the Nazis and the Communists.

In fact, as a youth, Pope John Paul II (then named Karol Wojtyla) entered a secret seminary, because the Church was repressed by the government. When he was a priest and a bishop in Poland, a hostile government was still in power, which meant he had to use every creative way possible to communicate his message wherever he could.

As a young priest, Father Wojtyla was sent to Rome to study for a doctoral degree in theology, so he could better explain the Faith to the Polish people. When he returned to Poland, he studied for another doctorate in philosophy, in order to explain even better the Catholic Faith.

As successor to St. Peter and as chief pastor of the universal Catholic Church, Pope John Paul II is the official teacher of all the Catholics of the world. He brings his rich educational background to his office as teacher, but he is also guided by the Holy Spirit as he teaches in the name of Christ.

◆

Even though he is the supreme teacher of the Catholic Faith, Pope John Paul II meets regularly with the other bishops of the world to encourage them as teachers of the Faith. The Pope knows that he is the successor of Peter, the leader of the Apostles, but he understands that the bishops are the successors of the Apostles, who were also sent to proclaim and teach the "Good News" of Jesus' message.

Pope John Paul II and the bishops form a college of bishops, of which he is the head. They work together, and he encourages bishops to be the best teachers of the Faith that they possibly can be in their local dioceses.

◆

One way a Pope can teach the faithful is by issuing an encyclical, an official letter to teach and explain the Faith. These letters are held in high regard by Catholics, because they help Catholics better understand the importance of specific teachings of the Faith. Pope John Paul II has issued encyclicals on a number of points of the Faith, such as those regarding Jesus Christ, God's mercy, the Holy Spirit, the Blessed Virgin Mary, social justice issues, and the Christian understanding of work.

In order to ensure that the Tradition of the Faith is handed on, the Pope also explains and continues teaching truths of the Catholic Faith that have been taught by other Popes and Church councils. He does this in his many travels and in audiences at the Vatican.

Pope John Paul II knows what it means to be a good teacher. He knows that a good teacher loves his message and his listeners. Because of his love for the Faith and for all people, Pope John Paul II never misses an opportunity to spread and explain the Faith.

Mother Elizabeth Ann Seton: Founder of the First American Parish School

The following is an interview with Mother Elizabeth Ann Seton, who has started the first American parish school.

Reporter: Did you always have the desire to start a Catholic parish school?

Mother Seton: Certainly not. In God's Providence, a number of events paved the way. I was not even born a Catholic; I was brought up Episcopalian. So I certainly did not set out as a young person to start a Catholic school.

Reporter: What led to your becoming Catholic?

Mother Seton: As a young girl I was brought up in the late 1700s in New York by a very religious mother and, after she died, by a stepmother; both were Episcopalians. My father, Dr. Richard Bayley, was not very religious, but he taught me some good human values.

I later married a wealthy Episcopalian named William Magee Seton, and we had five children. He died of tuberculosis when I was thirty, and I was left in poverty because his business had floundered.

Before he died, I had gone with him to Italy, where I was exposed to the Catholic Faith. I was impressed by the Catholic belief in the Real Presence of Jesus in the Eucharist, by the Catholic devotion to Mary, and by the Catholic belief that their Church is the Church of Christ and the Apostles.

Shortly after my husband's death, I became a Catholic.

Reporter: Did your friends and family accept your decision to become Catholic?

Mother Seton: Many of them did not. It was a difficult period of my life. I was a widow with five children, and I had to open a school to support myself and family.

Reporter: Was that the first Catholic parish school?

Mother Seton: No. Shortly after that I was asked by the Bishop of Baltimore to come to Maryland to start a Catholic school. I honored his request, and eventually I started a religious community of women. I still had children whom I was raising, but the bishop gave me permission to start the community, which we called "Sisters of Charity".

Reporter: What is the most important thing you have done?

Mother Seton: The will of God. Sometimes, I may prefer to do other things, but doing the will of God is most important. Once I told my religious sisters, "The first end I propose in our daily work is to do the will of God; secondly, to do it in the manner He wills it; and thirdly, to do it because it is His will."

Source: *Saint of the Day,* p. 7.

John Baptist de la Salle: Founder of the Brothers of the Christian Schools

ROUEN, FRANCE (1717) – A great leader in education has influenced Catholic education in France during the past number of years, and his new order is now growing beyond the confines of this country. Father John Baptist de la Salle has brought men together to form a religious community of brothers to be teachers in many schools in this country.

As a young priest in Rheims in 1679, John Baptist de la Salle started as a canon, a priest assigned to the cathedral. Canon de la Salle met a man by the name of Adrian Nyel, who came to Rheims to start a school for poor boys.

The young canon became interested in Nyel's work and helped the teachers with his own money. He eventually invited seven teachers to live with him, but five soon left, because they could not live with the discipline he expected of them. Then other men joined Canon de la Salle, and his movement grew.

Because Canon de la Salle became very involved in this work and because he wanted to live a more simple life, he gave up his position as canon. He possessed a private fortune, but he gave all his money to the poor.

Soon after that, Father de la Salle organized the teachers into a community of brothers, who were called the Brothers of the Christian Schools. Eventually, young boys between the ages of fifteen and twenty began to apply to this community, so Father de la Salle set up a junior novitiate to prepare them to become brothers.

Other men came to Father de la Salle, sent by parish priests to be trained as teachers and to return to their own villages. In 1687, Father de la Salle founded a college in Rheims for educating teachers.

In 1698, James II, the exiled former king of England, requested that the Brothers establish a college for Irish boys from wealthy families. This was a change in the community's policy of teaching only poor children. By 1700, brothers in the community were being sent to Rome and to towns throughout France. The rule of Father de la Salle's order stated that its members would be brothers and not ordained priests.

As a teacher of the Faith, Father de la Salle has experienced many disappointments and also resistance from lay schoolmasters. In spite of these difficulties, the order founded by Father John Baptist de la Salle has continued serving the Church in the education of young people.

Sources: *Butler's Lives of the Saints*; *Saint of the Day*; *The Work Is Yours.*

Angela Merici: Organizer of Women Teachers

BRESCIA, ITALY (1539) – Angela Merici is a woman determined to help teach the Faith to young girls, particularly poor girls, and she has organized twenty-seven other women into an association to help accomplish her goals.

This group of women, founded under the protection of St. Ursula, is not a religious order. The women live in their homes and do not wear any special religious habit. They do not take vows of poverty, chastity, and obedience, but they are asked to live a life that embraces these practices.

After Angela's parents died when she was ten years old, she was raised by an uncle. At about the age of twenty-two, Angela retrned to Desenzano, the town of her birth. When she saw that many of the poorer children in Desenzano knew little about their Catholic Faith, she set out to teach them, with the assistance of other women.

Angela was later asked to come here to Brescia to open a school, which she did. In 1525, when she visited Rome, Pope Clement VII suggested that she take charge of a group of nursing sisters there, but she declined the offer and returned to Brescia.

Shortly afterward, war forced her to move to Cremona. After the war, she returned to Brescia to the delight of its citizens, who have a high regard for her charity and holiness.

The community originally founded by Angela Marici was an "association", but eventually it developed into a religious order.

John Bosco: Teacher of Youth

TURIN, ITALY (1859) – Father John Bosco has banded together a group of twenty-two men to devote their lives to working with young people. They have organized under the title of Salesians, in honor of St. Francis de Sales, and Pope Pius IX has recently approved their rules.

Working with youth is not something new for Father Bosco. As a young boy himself, he had a dream in which he was trying to calm a group of unruly children. In the dream a mysterious lady said to him, "Softly, softly . . . if you wish to win them! Take your shepherd's staff and lead them to pasture." The children in the dream turned first into beasts and then into young sheep.

After that dream, young John Bosco worked with poor boys, catechizing them, taking them to church, and sometimes entertaining them with acrobatics and tricks.

Even during his seminary years, John Bosco worked with young children of the city. His first appointment as a priest was to be chaplain of a girls' school, and in his free time he worked with young boys.

Father Bosco recently founded a trade school in which destitute boys learn to become apprentices. Father Bosco considers this school his greatest accomplishment to date.

ASSIGNMENT

Interviewing a Saint

Look through a book of the lives of the saints and choose a saint who is noted for spreading the Faith by teaching. Write a newspaper interview based on the information you have read in this book. You may want to consult several such books or a biography of the saint.

As you put together the interview, you may want to ask some of the same questions used in the interviewing exercise earlier in this chapter. See if you can find the answers to these questions as you do your reading and put together your interview. If you find quotations from your saint, you may want to use them in your interview, making sure to identify your source.

Remember that the purpose of these interviews is to find out how the saints spread the Faith by their words. In this chapter we are focusing on the gift of the Holy Spirit bestowed upon us to help us to spread the Faith by our words.

Prayers and Teachings Every Catholic Should Know

On this page is a list of prayers and teachings that every Catholic should know about the Faith. The Holy Spirit is given in the sacrament of Confirmation to help you spread and defend the Catholic Faith. To explain the Catholic Faith to someone, you must know some of the basic teachings and prayers of the Catholic religion. A person who does not know some of the important teachings and prayers of the Faith will find it difficult to spread and defend that Faith.

You should memorize these prayers and teachings before Confirmation. Confirmation is not meant to be a reward for knowing certain aspects of the Faith, but you should have a certain level of competency in the Faith before being sent by the Church to explain and defend it.

It is important that you first have a level of competency appropriate to your age, so that once the gift of the Holy Spirit is given, you may use the gifts the Holy Spirit bestows, in an appropriate and intelligent manner.

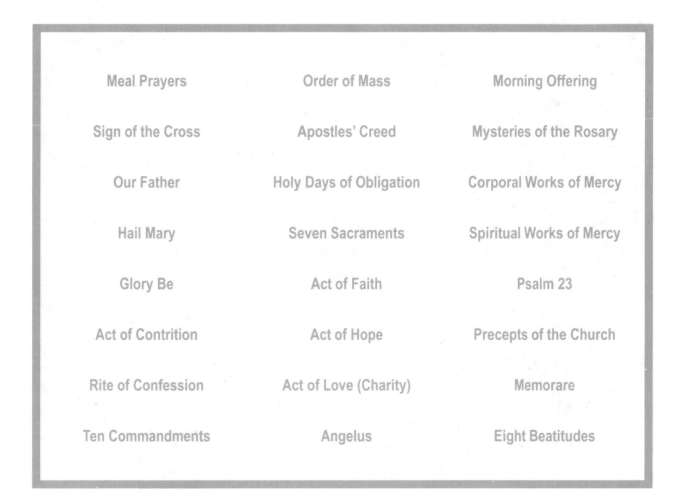

Meal Prayers	Order of Mass	Morning Offering
Sign of the Cross	Apostles' Creed	Mysteries of the Rosary
Our Father	Holy Days of Obligation	Corporal Works of Mercy
Hail Mary	Seven Sacraments	Spiritual Works of Mercy
Glory Be	Act of Faith	Psalm 23
Act of Contrition	Act of Hope	Precepts of the Church
Rite of Confession	Act of Love (Charity)	Memorare
Ten Commandments	Angelus	Eight Beatitudes

5 DEFENDING THE FAITH

The Holy Spirit is given to us at Confirmation not only to spread the Catholic Faith, but also to defend it. In Baptism, we were made prophets, that is, heralds of the Good News; and in Confirmation, the Holy Spirit enlivens our prophetic calling. As prophets, we must be willing to defend the message of Christ against the attacks of those who defame or distort the truths of God.

In Confirmation, the Holy Spirit deepens in us His seven gifts of wisdom, understanding, knowledge, fortitude, counsel, piety, and fear of the Lord. The Holy Spirit gives us the gifts of the mind—wisdom, understanding, knowledge, and counsel—to help us to know what to say in defense of the Faith.

The Holy Spirit also deepens in us the gift of fortitude (or courage) to be able to stand up to the those who defame and ridicule the Faith. To be courageous is to have governance of one's self, to have control of one's self in the face of fear. Without this gift of the Holy Spirit, we might shrink away from the forces of evil, but with it we can stand up to the world, the flesh, and the devil. We are given the strength to defend the Faith by what we say and by what we do.

The sacrament of Confirmation makes you a defender of the Faith, a kind of "soldier of Christ". A soldier is a person who has courage and strength to defend his country. Soldiers are willing to ward off the enemy even if doing so may mean their own death. The "soldier of Christ" has been given the strength and courage to defend the Faith, even to the point of physical death, that is, martyrdom.

> *Our Lord Himself said before Pilate that He came to testify to the truth. Those who opposed Him crucified Him. We can expect to suffer when we testify to the truth. It is the Holy Spirit Who will give us courage to face our opposition.*

Let us examine some news stories about individuals who have defended and suffered for the sake of God's word, even to the extent of dying for the Faith.

Jeremiah—A Persecuted Prophet

One of the men in Judea who is decrying false worship (idolatry) in the country is Jeremiah. He was born of a priestly family in the village of Anathoth. As a prophet, he had upheld the reform efforts of King Josiah.

Since the fall of Josiah, Jeremiah has been speaking out against idolatry and has been beaten, imprisoned, and thrown into a cistern, where he sank in the mud. When questioned about his objections, Jeremiah explained that during Josiah's rule the abuses of religion were being corrected, but since Josiah's death many abuses have started up again.

Looking upon himself as a religious reformer who has been called by God to decry these abuses, Jeremiah adamantly has spoken out against the pagan gods being worshiped in Judea. He has warned that if the people of Judea do not reform their lives, they will suffer the serious consequences of abandoning the true God and His care.

Dominic—Defender of the Faith

TOULOUSE, FRANCE (1220) – A new order of Friar Preachers has begun recently under the leadership of a priest by the name of Father Dominic. We interviewed Father Dominic in order to learn more about the founder of this order.

Question: How did you begin your order?
Father Dominic: It's a long story. As a young man I studied for the priesthood, and I was going to be a canon at the Cathedral in Osma, Spain. I was intending to spend most of my life in prayer.

After I was ordained, the bishop took me on a trip to other parts of Europe, where I saw how the Albigensian heresy was affecting the Church. I decided I should try to fight this heresy through preaching.

Question: What is the Albigensian heresy?
Father Dominic: Its proponents say that all material things are evil, even the human body. Therefore, they say, Jesus could not have become a man. Furthermore, they are teaching that God could not work through sacraments, because they are material signs. The Albigensians are leading very rigorous lives, so the common people are impressed with them. On the other hand, the people are not impressed with Catholic preachers speaking against Albigensianism, because many of them are living lives of luxury.

Question: What have you done?
Father Dominic: I gathered together three Cistercian monks, and we have begun to go around preaching. We are also trying to live a very simple life. With God's grace, our preaching and example are helping to bring many Albigensians back to the Catholic Faith.

Question: Was this preaching the beginning of your order?
Father Dominic: In a sense, it was, for eventually some of those who were preaching began to form a community.

Question: What is the ideal of your order?
Father Dominic: The ideal is to combine the contemplative (prayer) life with the active life. I tell the Friars that they are "to speak only of God or with God". This means prayer, study, and preaching the word of God.

Sources: *Saint of the Day*; *Butler's Lives of the Saints*.

THOMAS MORE EXECUTED

LONDON (June 6, 1535) – Thomas More, former chancellor of England, was beheaded today for refusing to swear to the Oath of Supremacy. Having recently been charged with treason, More had been imprisoned in the Tower of London while he awaited trial.

More had opposed King Henry VIII's divorce of his first wife, Catherine, and his recent marriage to Anne Boleyn. Over the years, More had been the King's close friend, but he refused to approve these actions because of the Church's teaching against divorce and remarriage.

King Henry has recently declared himself supreme head of the Church of England. The king, therefore, denied that he was subject to the authority of the Pope in Rome, who refused to grant an annulment of the king's marriage to Catherine. More had an unswerving allegiance to the Pope, whom he believed to be the successor of the Apostle Peter.

More, who was known to be a man of great faith, had been a scholar, a lawyer, a husband, and the father of four children.

Paul—Apostle to the Gentiles

ROME (67) – One of the leaders of the new religious movement called Christianity is awaiting trial in Rome. His title is "Apostle", and his Christian name is Paul. Before he converted from Judaism to Christianity, he was known as Saul of Tarsus.

In an interview Paul described his travels through the Mediterranean area preaching about Jesus, the founder of the new religion. He explained that the message of Jesus was being preached only to Jews, until God made known to the followers of Jesus that the message was to be proclaimed to all people of all nations.

"I have been involved in this effort to bring the Gospel to other people as well as the Jews", Paul said. "Some of the early Christians did not want the message to be preached to non-Jews, so I presented my case to a council in Jerusalem, at which Peter, the head of the Church, spoke and confirmed that Gentiles should indeed have the Gospel preached to them.

"Because I was the one who brought this matter to the Church, I have become known as the "Apostle to the Gentiles", he explained. "But preaching the Good News to all nations has not been an easy task. I have had to endure many hardships in preaching the Gospel.

"At one point, in a place by the name of Lystra, I was stoned and left for dead, but my companion, Barnabas, and I escaped from the area. In Philippi, another companion, Silas, and I were beaten and imprisoned, but we were set free by a miracle."

Paul was also arrested in Jerusalem, but he was transferred to Caesarea, where he was held for two years while a trial continued. Because Paul was a Roman citizen, he demanded a trial by the emperor and was sent by ship to Rome. During the voyage, the ship was wrecked at Malta. He was finally brought here to Rome, however, where he is currently awaiting trial.

Ignatius of Antioch Condemned to Death

TROAS, ASIA MINOR (107) – Ignatius, a bishop of the Catholic Church from the city of Antioch, has been condemned to death in Rome. He was interviewed here in Troas as he was en route to Rome.

Question: Why have you been sentenced to death?
Bishop Ignatius: Because I refused to worship the Emperor, whom the Romans believe to be divine, I am considered to be a traitor, and treason is punishable by death.
Question: Aren't your actions extreme? Isn't your life important?
Bishop Ignatius: My life is important, because it is a gift from God. But my life was given to me by God to know and love Him. If I deny Him, I will betray the One Who has created me to love Him. I can never turn my back upon my Creator.
Question: Are you afraid of death?
Bishop Ignatius: I look forward to meeting my Creator. I know that I will continue to live with God for all eternity. In fact, I wrote to the Christians in Rome and said, "I am God's wheat and shall be ground by the wild beast's teeth so that I may become Christ's pure bread."
Question: Have you any concerns as you go to your death?
Bishop Ignatius: As a bishop, I am concerned for other Christians that they remain faithful to Jesus. I have written letters to them, pleading that they be true to their baptismal promises. I also encouraged them to be obedient to their bishops, for bishops are the successors of the Apostles to whom Jesus entrusted His Church. I am also concerned that they not follow any false doctrines but only the teachings of Christ as presented by the Church.

Source: *Saint of the Day.*

Knowledge to Defend the Faith

The Holy Spirit is given to us in the sacrament of Confirmation so that we may spread and defend the Catholic Faith by what we say and do. You cannot speak intelligently concerning the Faith if you do not know the basic beliefs of the Catholic religion.

To help your understanding of the essential teachings of the Catholic Faith, review the list of definitions on the following pages. You should learn and be able to give the definition of each word on this list.

People who want to market or sell a product do not stop learning about the product. Their company gives them certain basic background information before they begin to sell, but they continue to learn more and more about the product, so that they can answer questions and explain every possible aspect concerning it.

Sales and marketing personnel also look for opportunities to introduce other people to the product. Often in a conversation or social gathering they will seek an opening to talk a little bit about the product. How much more so should it be with you who make the Catholic Faith known to others. You should seek appropriate opportunities to explain the Faith. You could make a simple statement to a friend or acquaintance, such as, "I'll pray for you." In such an instance, at least the other person will know that you believe God is in control and not just us. In addition, there may be an opportunity to explain a sacrament or an occasion to defend the Faith against some derogatory remark. In any event, you need to know the Catholic Faith well in order to explain or defend it.

The definitions given on the next two pages are not exhaustive, but merely a beginning. After you receive the sacrament of Confirmation you should continue your study of the Faith. The more you know and understand, the better you will be able to explain and defend Christ, His teachings, and the Catholic Church. Also, the more you understand, the more people will come on their own to you to seek information about the Faith. People look for persons who are knowledgeable about particular fields of endeavor. Just as when we have a problem with an automobile or computer we seek out people who are knowledgeable about them, so too, individuals who are searching for answers about their Faith will come to us, if we are able to explain the Catholic Faith.

DEFINITIONS FOR A CATHOLIC WHO CAN DEFEND THE FAITH

God: the all-powerful, almighty, all-knowing, and eternal Being, Who created the universe.

Trinity: the term used to describe three Persons (Father, Son, and Holy Spirit) in one God.

God the Father: the first Person of the Blessed Trinity; from God the Father proceeds God the Son and God the Holy Spirit, Who proceeds from both the Father and the Son.

Jesus Christ: the Second Person of the Trinity, Who became Man, and Who has both a divine and a human nature but is one divine Person.

Holy Spirit: the Third Person of the Blessed Trinity, Who is equal to the Father and the Son.

Incarnation: the term used for the Second Person of God becoming Man.

Blessed Virgin Mary: the virgin Mother of Jesus, the Second Person of God Who was both God and Man.

Annunciation: the event in which the Archangel Gabriel announced to Mary that God wanted her to be the Mother of His Son.

Visitation: Mary's visit to her cousin Elizabeth after Mary learns she is to be the Mother of God.

Nativity: Jesus' birth in Bethlehem.

Crucifixion: Jesus' death on the Cross on Good Friday.

Resurrection: Jesus' rising from the dead on Easter morning, the third day after His death.

Ascension: Jesus' returning to heaven to be with His Heavenly Father forty days after His Resurrection.

Immaculate Conception: Mary's being free of original sin from the time of her conception in the womb of her mother, St. Anne.

Assumption: Mary's being taken into Heaven, body and soul, when her earthly life was over.

redemption: the act of God merited by Jesus' death and Resurrection that freed us from sin and some of the effects of sin.

salvation: our being saved from sin, death, and hell by the merits of Jesus Christ's death and Resurrection.

grace: the spiritual gift from God that is unmerited by us and that brings us closer to God and enables us to remain faithful to Him; God's life in us.

sanctifying grace: the spiritual gift from God that enables us to share in His life and to become holy like Him.

actual grace: a spiritual gift from God that helps us to know and love God and our neighbor.

soul: the invisible, spiritual, and immortal gift from God that gives us life.

angels: spiritual persons created by God with a will and intellect but no body, who enjoy the Beatific Vision of God and help us to attain heaven.

devils: spiritual persons created by God with a will and intellect but no body; they have rejected God and suffer in hell; they seek our sinful rejection of God.

Old Testament: the first part of the Bible, written before the coming of Jesus Christ.

New Testament: the second part of the Bible, written after the death and Resurrection of Jesus Christ.

liturgy: the official, public prayers and rites of the Church, particularly the Holy Sacrifice of the Mass.

sacrament: a physical sign, given to us by Jesus, through which Jesus meets us and gives us grace.

Baptism: the sacrament in which by water and the gift of the Holy Spirit we are made adopted sons and daughters of God, members of the Church, and heirs of heaven.

baptismal character: a change in us, caused by the sacrament of Baptism, that makes us more like Christ in a permanent, indelible way. Because of the baptismal character, one is made capable of receiving the other sacraments.

Confirmation: the sacrament by which a person is anointed on the forehead with oil and is thereby strengthened by the gift of the Holy Spirit to spread and defend the Catholic Faith by word and deed.

confirmation character: a change in us, caused by the sacrament of Confirmation, that makes us more like Christ in a permanent way. Because of the confirmation character, one is made capable of spreading and defending the Catholic Faith in a mature way.

Eucharist: the sacrament in which Jesus gives Himself body and soul, divinity and humanity, to us under the appearance of bread and wine that have been changed into His Body and Blood.

transsubstantiation: the term used to indicate that at the Consecration of the Mass the bread and wine become a new substance, namely, the Body and Blood of Jesus Christ.

Reconciliation: the sacrament whereby we confess our sins with sorrow in our hearts to a priest who, as the representative of Christ and the Church, forgives them.

Anointing of the Sick: the sacrament in which a priest anoints the head and hands of a seriously sick or very elderly person, and Christ gives strength to help the person spiritually and sometimes physically, if it be God's will for the person to recover.

Holy Orders: the sacrament in which a man becomes a bishop, priest, or deacon and receives the powers of that office.

Matrimony: the sacrament in which a baptized man and a baptized woman promise to take one another to be husband and wife, and through their permanent, faithful, and fruitful love become a sign of Christ's love for the Church.

Eucharistic Sacrifice: the Sacrifice of Jesus' death on the Cross made present in an unbloody manner at the Consecration of the Mass, so that we can worship the Father and offer our own sacrifices with this great Sacrifice of the Lord.

Pope (Holy Father): the successor to St. Peter who, as Bishop of Rome and head of the college of bishops, is pastor of the universal Catholic Church and teaches, sanctifies, and governs all Catholics.

bishop: a successor to the Apostles, who is pastor of a diocese. He teaches, sanctifies, and governs in the name of Christ, and, with the other bishops of the world in union with the Pope, teaches the entire Church.

infallibility: the gift given by the Holy Spirit to the Church that it might be free from error concerning truths of Faith and morals necessary for our salvation. This gift is given especially to the Magisterium.

Catholic Church: the Church founded by Jesus Christ, which continues the fullness of Christ's teachings and the seven sacraments.

divine revelation: the hidden truths that God chose to reveal about Himself.

Tradition: A "handing on" of all God's revelation from the beginning of human history to the end of the apostolic age. It includes all of Sacred Scripture and the words, life, and actions of Jesus Christ, whether these have been written down or transmitted orally. Tradition is passed on from one generation of believers to the next. Tradition is preserved under the guidance of the Holy Spirit through the Church founded by Christ.

Sacred Scripture (Bible): that message of salvation given by God to the Church, which has been written down under the inspiration of the Holy Spirit.

mystery: a truth that cannot be fully understood by man.

heaven: the place where those who have died in the state of sanctifying grace will receive the rewards of everlasting life, particularly the happiness of seeing God face-to-face.

Purgatory: the state in which those who have died in the state of sanctifying grace are purified of the effects of sin, so they can enjoy heaven for all eternity.

hell: the place where those who have died in the state of mortal sin will suffer for all eternity, particularly because of being separated from God.

absolution: the action of the priest in the sacrament of Reconciliation whereby, as a representative of Jesus and His Church, he forgives sins.

conscience: the interior faculty that enables us to decide what is right or wrong in a particular situation.

firm purpose of amendment: the decision, with the help of God's grace, not to sin again.

examination of conscience: a review of how I have been faithful to God's will and commands.

original sin: the first sin committed by Adam and Eve. We inherit original sin from Adam and Eve, which means that we are conceived and born without grace. Without grace, we cannot share God's life on earth and we cannot live with God in heaven.

mortal sin: a thought, word, deed, or an omission of a deed, that offends God so grievously that it cuts us off from the friendship of God.

venial sin: a thought, word, deed, or an omission of a deed, that offends God but does not break our friendship with Him.

pastor: the priest who has been put in charge of a parish.

deacon: a man ordained to be of service in the Church and who can baptize, witness marriages, assist at the Eucharist, preach, and bury the dead.

laity (lay people): the non-ordained, baptized members of the Church.

diocese: a geographical territory of the Church under the authority of a bishop.

cardinal: an honorary title given usually to a bishop. A cardinal has the privilege of electing a Pope and is occasionally consulted by the Pope on special matters.

ecumenism: prayer and cooperation between Christian churches to understand better one another's beliefs and practices and to foster the unity of all believers, for which Jesus prayed at His Last Supper.

sacramental: a prayer, object, or action that helps us to become closer to God through the disposition of the one using it, rather than the rite being used.

Always Be Ready to Give an Explanation

In a letter addressed to the Gentile churches of Asia Minor, the author writes, "Always be ready to give an explanation to anyone who asks you a reason for your hope" (1 Pt 3:15). Being a Catholic should not mean merely having been born into a Catholic family. A Catholic should live the Catholic Faith and be able to give reasons for believing in Christ and His Church. A mature Catholic should be able to give intelligent reasons for being Catholic.

When someone who is not a believer attacks or ridicules the Faith, Catholics should be able to explain why they are Catholic. If you are well-versed in the Faith, you will be better able to answer objections to the Faith. You should be able to listen to objections to the Faith and have the confidence to answer these objections. Your task is to deepen your understanding of the Faith, so as to be able to answer any difficulties or objections.

Apologetics is the name we give to the study of defending the Faith. It presents reasons for believing in Christ and His Church. These reasons will probably not produce an act of faith on the part of a non-believer, but they will point an individual in the direction of the Faith.

ASSIGNMENT

Practice for Defending the Faith

The following questions are commonly asked by people who misunderstand the Catholic Faith. These questions can sometimes be presented in a challenging manner. An intelligent Catholic is able to defend the truths that have been handed on to us from Christ and His Apostles. Write one or two paragraphs in answer to each of the following questions.

Question 1 I believe in God, but why do I have to go to Church on Sunday?

Question 2 I believe in Jesus, but why should a person be a Catholic? Isn't one Christian religion as good as the next?

Question 3 I want to be a free person. Why does the Catholic Church have so many rules?

Question 4 A woman should have a right to her own body. Why does the Church teach that a woman cannot have an abortion?

Satan Continues to Tempt Us

Even now, Satan, as a devil, continues to tempt people to disobey God. Because of his superior intelligence, no one can come close to outwitting him. He is sly and the father of all lies.

If we think that we can surpass the intelligence and cunning of Satan, we are sorely mistaken, and Satan has already outwitted us by letting us think that we can outsmart him. How, then, can we overcome the temptations of Satan?

By God's grace. It is only through the power of the death and Resurrection of Jesus that we are able to overcome the temptations of Satan. We should pray hard when we are tempted to sin.

If we have given in to Satan's temptations, we should turn away from Satan and sin by turning toward Christ in the sacrament of Reconciliation. We should receive both the sacraments of Reconciliation and the Eucharist frequently to become strong in our Faith.

The sacrament of Confirmation also will give us the strength to withstand the trials and temptations placed in our lives through the workings of Satan. The Holy Spirit will strengthen us in the seven gifts of wisdom, understanding, knowledge, counsel, fortitude, piety, and fear of the Lord to fight against Satan.

When we overcome the sin in our lives, we become examples of virtue for others. Our light shines so that others can see the goodness of God. We, then, become witnesses to Jesus by what we say and do. The mission of the Holy Spirit in Confirmation is accomplished. We spread the Faith by our words and actions.

Satan was an angel of God with the highest intelligence. Shortly after he was created, Satan was given the choice to serve God or not to serve Him.

In his pride, Satan decided not to serve God. That decision meant that Satan chose to live in separation from God forever in hell. Still, Satan battled to take over heaven. Michael, an archangel in heaven, defeated Satan, and Satan now reigns in hell.

Prayer to St. Michael the Archangel

St. Michael, the Archangel, defend us in battle,
be our protection against the wickedness and snares of the devil;
may God rebuke him, we humbly pray,
and do thou, O Prince of the heavenly host, by the power of God,
thrust into hell Satan and all evil spirits
who wander through the world for the ruin of souls.
Amen.

Putting on the Armor of God

The Screwtape Letters

C. S. Lewis was a Christian author who wrote a series of imaginative letters from a master devil to a student devil. Screwtape is the master devil who instructs his nephew Wormwood, a student devil, in methods of tempting people. Screwtape understands human beings quite well and knows how easily they fall prey to temptations. Screwtape frequently refers to God as the "Enemy".

Even though C. S. Lewis uses imaginary characters, readers of these letters have an opportunity to reflect on the fact that devils do exist, and that they are our enemies and God's. Readers also can see that they should be on guard and pray, because humans are weak, and devils seek to destroy humanity.

Read Ephesians 6:10–17.

St. Paul wrote this letter from prison to the Christians at Ephesus, encouraging them to put on the "armor of God". In St. Paul's time, soldiers used armor to protect themselves in battle. St. Paul is keenly aware that the followers of Christ must be protected "against the tactics of the devil".

The armor of a Christian does not consist in shields, helmets, or swords, but in spiritual armor, because, as St. Paul wrote, "our struggle is not with flesh and blood but with the principalities, with the powers, with the world rulers of this present darkness, with the evil spirits in the heavens."

St. Paul wrote that the armor we should use is truth, righteousness (justice), and readiness (zeal) for the gospel of peace. We should "hold faith as a shield . . . . And take the helmet of salvation and the sword of the Spirit, which is the word of God."

St. Paul is aware that the power of evil must be resisted and that this power is something that should be taken seriously. The devil is in the world and anxious to tempt us to sin. We must resist him.

The Holy Spirit, in the sacrament of Confirmation, strengthens us in our battle against the devil. He strengthens us in our understanding of the truth and our readiness for bringing the Gospel to others. Our Faith is also bolstered.

The devil's goal is to keep people from knowing and loving God. The Holy Spirit is given in Confirmation to help us bring the Good News to others, that is, to help us counteract the devil's goal. We will be confronting the power of the devil as he seeks to destroy our efforts in leading others to Jesus and His Church. We are strengthened in our battle against him, and we have nothing to fear. Jesus, Who has overcome the powers of the devil by His death and Resurrection, has sent the Holy Spirit to help us.

ASSIGNMENT

Defending the Faith

Interview someone whose life has exhibited qualities that a defender of the Faith should possess. Choose the person from one of the following categories: a soldier (or someone who formerly served in the armed forces), an attorney, a former prisoner-of-war.

The positive qualities of character that a soldier, attorney, or prisoner-of-war may exhibit can point to the qualities needed to defend the Faith. By studying these positive qualities, we can understand better the qualities that a baptized and confirmed person needs to be a prophet for God. It is God's grace that enables us to defend the Faith.

For instance, a soldier must be brave and strong to defend his country. Similarly, a "soldier of Christ" must have courage (a gift of the Holy Spirit) and be spiritually strong to defend Christ and His teachings. An attorney must be prepared with knowledge of the law before beginning a defense in the courtroom. Similarly, a defender of the Faith must have the gifts of wisdom, knowledge, understanding, and counsel in order to defend Christ and His Church. A person who was detained as a prisoner of war endured hardships from persecutors. Likewise, someone who has received the sacrament of Confirmation must be willing to suffer for the sake of Christ, even to the point of death.

The following are examples of questions that could be asked:

For the soldier (or former member of the armed services):

1. What kind of training did you have to undergo to prepare yourself to be a member of the armed services? Did this training help you to become stronger physically? Did it help you to become more courageous?
2. Did you ever have to fight in a battle?
3. Were you afraid to fight? How did you overcome your fears?
4. Were you ever injured in battle?
5. Did you have a sense of purpose of protecting your country while you were in the armed services?

For the attorney:

1. What kind of education did you have to become an attorney? How many years did you have to go to school?
2. What skills are needed to defend someone in the courtroom?
3. What kind of preparation do you do for a court case?
4. What kinds of difficulties do you encounter when you are defending someone?
5. Have you ever been afraid as you have entered a courtroom? What do you do when you are afraid?`

For a former prisoner of war:

1. Why were you placed in a detention camp?
2. What were the conditions under which you lived?
3. Did you suffer much? What kinds of suffering did you endure? Did anyone ever die in the detention camp while you were there?
4. Were you ever afraid for your life in the detention camp?
5. What made you strong as you suffered?

6 SPREADING THE FAITH

In the sacrament of Confirmation we receive the Holy Spirit in a special way so that we can spread and defend the Faith by what we say and do. In this chapter we will focus on spreading the Faith by our actions, particularly through service to God and others.

You have probably heard people say "Actions speak louder than words." In many instances that is true. Even though we need the written and spoken word to help us know Who God is and what is truly good, many times we are inspired to pursue God and what is good by the example of others.

Jesus became a servant to others . . .

Our actions express who we are—followers of Jesus Christ. Our good deeds give witness to others, so that those who know us can see a reflection of the Lord's goodness in our actions.

In our Baptism we began to share in the kingly office of Jesus Christ. As king, Jesus became a servant to others by disciplining Himself and using the things of this world for the benefit of others. In doing this, Jesus spread the Gospel. The kingly office enables us to become servants to others by disciplining ourselves and using the things of this world for the benefit of others. In doing this we imitate Christ, the King, and we are enabled to spread the Gospel. In Confirmation we are strengthened in the kingly office.

In this chapter we can view the lives of some great people who witnessed to their Faith by serving God and others.

Mother Frances Cabrini—Italian Missionary to the United States

CHICAGO (1917) – Even though as a child Mother Cabrini had a fear of drowning, she has made almost thirty sea voyages to pursue the work to which she has been called. And that work is to care for the poor, the infirm, the destitute, and the uneducated.

Born in Italy in 1850, she began her works of service at an orphanage in her homeland. When the orphanage was closed by the local bishop, she was named prioress of the Missionary Sisters of the Sacred Heart.

Although she expressed a desire to go to China as a missionary, Pope Leo XIII urged her to go to the United States. She went to New York City with several other sisters to open an orphanage there.

She arrived in New York in 1889 to find that the building for her orphanage could not be used. This disappointment did not stop her. She stayed and finally found a way to open the orphanage. She went on to open more than fifty other institutions of service throughout the Western Hemisphere.

Mother Cabrini has helped people of many national backgrounds. However, being Italian, Mother Cabrini has focused on helping Italian immigrants in the United States. During the course of her work, she became a naturalized citizen of the United States.

Sources: *Butler's Lives of the Saints*; *Saint of the Day*.

VINCENT DE PAUL
Priest of the Poor

PARIS (1660) – Father Vincent de Paul is now well known in France for his work with the poor. However, he has not always been engaged in helping the poor. At the beginning of his ordained priesthood, he earned a comfortable living as one of the chaplains to the queen.

After hearing the deathbed confession of a servant, Father de Paul came to see the spiritual needs of peasants. Shortly after that experience, Father de Paul decided to join the priests who are now known as the Congregation of the Mission.

This new congregation consists of a group of priests who serve in small towns and villages, taking vows of poverty, chastity, obedience, and stability. After a period of working with this group of priests, Father de Paul became their leader.

Father de Paul has set up associations of charitable people to assist the needy of parishes. One of the people whom Father de Paul influenced through these associations is Sister Louise de Marillac. Sister Louise has helped to establish the Daughters of Charity (Sisters of Charity of St. Vincent de Paul).

Father de Paul has already accomplished many things—from setting up hospitals to helping to begin seminaries. He has freed galley slaves and motivated wealthy women to raise funds for the missions. But, in the midst of these great works, Father de Paul has understood that the virtue of charity was more than merely doing good works. Charity is the performance of good works out of love for God and neighbor.

Father de Paul once said to a religious sister who was making her first visit to the poor, "You will find that charity is a heavy burden to carry, heavier than the kettle of soup and the basket of bread. But you must keep your gentleness and your smile. Giving soup and bread isn't all; the rich can do that."

Father de Paul also understands the importance of God's grace in his life. He notes that he would have been a very tough person to deal with had it not been for God's grace softening his heart and making it responsive to others' needs.

Sources: *Saint of the Day; Butler's Lives of the Saints.*

Mother Teresa of Calcutta— A Witness to God's Love by Her Life

Mother Teresa of Calcutta is a person of action who started an order of religious women who help the poorest of the poor throughout the world.

She had been a Loreto nun teaching the daughters of the rich in India. While riding on a train on her way to make a retreat, she received a call from God to leave to others the work of teaching and to follow Jesus by helping the poor in the slums. With the permission of the Pope she began this work in 1948.

She first started a school for poor children and, shortly after, a home for the dying. This home gave shelter to sick people who would have died on the streets. Mother Teresa and sisters who joined her work brought the dying homeless to this home. The sisters made them feel wanted and loved. Through this care, the dying people could experience both human and divine love. Because of the care the sisters gave them, some of these people were able to survive.

In talking about her work with the poorest of the poor, Mother Teresa has said, "The work is only the expression of the love we have for God. We have to pour our love on someone. And the people are the means of expressing our love for God."

Mother Teresa's work has spread throughout the entire world, and her sisters are now also serving the poor in the United States, in such places as St. Louis, New York, Los Angeles, San Francisco, Washington, D.C., and Appalachia. Throughout the world their work has expanded to include children, unwed mothers, the elderly, lepers, and AIDS patients.

Even though Mother Teresa has helped people with many different diseases, she once said that being unwanted "is the worst disease that any human being can ever experience. Nowadays we have found medicine for leprosy and lepers can be cured. There's medicine for TB and consumptives can be cured.

"For all kinds of diseases there are medicines and cures", Mother Teresa continued. "But for being unwanted, except there are willing hands to serve and there's a loving heart to love, I don't think this terrible disease can ever be cured. This is what we are aiming at, to bring to the people the willing hands to serve and the hearts to go on loving them, and to look at them as Christ."

Sisters in the order Mother Teresa founded are called Missionaries of Charity. They take the three traditional vows of poverty, chastity, and obedience, but they also take a fourth vow of giving their "whole-hearted free service to the poorest of the poor—to Christ in his distressing disguise", explained Mother Teresa.

In commenting on the work of the sisters, Mother Teresa said, "We must be able to radiate the joy of Christ, express it in our actions. If our actions are just useful actions that give no joy to the people, our poor people would never be able to rise up to the call which we want them to hear, the call to come closer to God." She has also founded an order for men who serve the poorest of the poor.

Quotations are from Malcolm Muggeridge, *Something Beautiful for God* (New York: Harper & Row, 1971), pp. 97–99.

LEGATUS

Business Executives Taking Their Faith Seriously

"Legatus" is a Latin word meaning "ambassador", and it is the name of a new, international organization for Catholic CEO's (chief executive officers). The purpose of this organization is to help its members be witnesses in the world and servants of the Church. Members must be in charge of a corporation that has at least fifty full-time employees and a certain dollar level of annual sales, fees billed, or assets.

Members of Legatus meet monthly with an opportunity for the sacrament of Reconciliation, Mass, a social time, dinner, and a speaker or round-table discussion. The organization exists to assist its members in deepening their appreciation of the Catholic Faith and to explore creative ways to apply the Faith in their daily walks of life.

One member of Legatus recently helped a mission in Honduras. He invested more than one million dollars to aid this mission, building a church, setting up an agricultural program, establishing a banking system, assisting with a clothing factory, and aiding medical clinics. He also set up a program whereby the profits from several stores he owns in Central America will go to this mission.

This member of Legatus has not only helped the mission in Honduras. He has also helped with the building of the new cathedral in Managua, Nicaragua. This new cathedral is viewed as a symbol of reconstruction in a country whose moral character has deteriorated.

Members of Legatus are to take their Faith seriously. They are executives with talent and expertise in business and wealth, and they are using their gifts to serve the Lord and His Church and to assist others to do the same. One of the important objectives of the members of Legatus is to bring Christian values into the workplace.

ASSIGNMENT

Interviewing People of Service

People who have received the sacrament of Confirmation are to spread and defend the Faith by what they say and do. In focusing on the ways Catholics can witness to their Faith by what they do, you are to interview three Catholics to find out how they witness to their belief in Jesus and His Church through their actions. Choose from among parents, priests, deacons, religious sisters or brothers, teachers, sponsors, relatives, members of your parish, or outstanding Catholics whom you know.

After your interviews, write a feature article summarizing how these people give witness to the Faith by their actions. The person may have also spread the Faith by word, but the article should focus on actions.

You may want to ask some of the following questions:

1. Do you have a special calling in the Church?
2. What kind of work do you do?
3. How do you spread the Faith by your actions in your vocation or work?
4. Do you have other opportunities to give witness to Jesus and His Church outside your vocation or work? What are some of these opportunities? Do you consciously look for new opportunities to serve others in your life?
5. Are you ever rejected by those to whom you show your Christian charity? Have you been criticized or ridiculed by people whom you are not assisting?
6. Have you ever been afraid to help others? Why?
7. Do you think about how the gifts of the Holy Spirit, strengthened in the sacrament of Confirmation, help you in aiding others?
8. Do you rely on the sacraments to strengthen you for your good works? Do you ever pray that the Holy Spirit will guide and strengthen you as you give witness by your actions? Do you have a conscious appreciation of how prayer and the sacraments help you to be a witness to Christ and His Church and to grow in virtue?
9. Do any members of your religious community, family, parish, or friends encourage and support you in your good works? Do you see how your good works are subject to the authority of the Pope, the bishop, the head of your religious community, or the pastor?
10. Have there been times when your work has not gone well? Are there occasions when you have thought that your work, in cooperation with God's grace, has gone very well? Have you ever thought that God has worked through you to bring others closer to Him?
11. Do you ever have the opportunity to explain why you are doing your good actions? Do you ever have the opportunity to explain the Faith to those whom you are helping?

INTERVIEWING A SAINT

The saints lived heroic lives of doing acts of service for God and others. They provide us with examples of how we can be people of service, charity, and obedience to God's commandments and people who express the Faith by what we do.

Choose one saint and write a newspaper feature article based on that saint's life. Show how the saint spread the Faith through action, using the interview questions found in the assignment described at left. Answers to these questions will provide a good basis for the article. You may want to consult reference material available in your school or parish library. The reference material may contain quotations that you can use in your article.

Remember that the goal of this particular article is to point out how the saint spread the Faith through action. The saint may have also spread the Faith by word, but the article should focus on action.

Fortitude, Piety, and Fear of the Lord: Gifts of the Holy Spirit for Our Wills

The seven gifts of the Holy Spirit are given in Baptism, and they are deepened and strengthened in the sacrament of Confirmation. The Holy Spirit strengthens these gifts in us so that we can spread and defend the Faith by what we say and do.

In Chapter 4, we learned how wisdom, understanding, knowledge, and counsel assist our minds to help us spread and defend the Faith by what we say. In this chapter, we are focusing on fortitude, piety, and fear of the Lord, because they assist our wills. In order to give witness by what we do, we involve our wills by seeking that which we know to be good and by loving God and our neighbor.

Fortitude (or courage) is the gift of the Holy Spirit that supports the will in loving God and our neighbor in the face of difficulty, even to the point of death or martyrdom. The Holy Spirit gives us the resolve to persevere in love of God and neighbor in the face of suffering. Fortitude also helps us to curb the fears that can keep us from doing good actions. This virtue moderates our actions so that we will not become reckless and try to face difficulties on our own, without the spiritual help we need to do good.

Piety (reverence) is the gift that enables us to hold God in the highest regard, because He created us and keeps us in His care. Piety is extended to our parents, relatives, and country. Piety also helps us to show reverence to our brothers and sisters in Christ, because they are sons and daughters of our Heavenly Father. Because we have this reverence for God and others, we treat God and holy things with respect. Piety also helps us to act justly toward all people and to help them in their need.

Fear of the Lord is a gift of the Holy Spirit that enables us to fear offending God because we do not want to offend the One who loves us so deeply. When we truly love someone, we do not want to offend that person and spoil our friendship. Fear of the Lord replaces a fear that serious sin will lose us heaven with a fear that our sin will offend God, Whom we love. This gift of the Holy Spirit, then, helps us to keep God's commandments as our response to the love of the Father, Son, and Holy Spirit. Fear of the Lord does not mean we are afraid of God. Rather, fear of the Lord helps us to have reverence for God and to respect Him.

As we use these gifts of the Holy Spirit, strengthened in the sacrament of Confirmation, they will help us to be witnesses to the Faith by what we do. They will also enable us to build up the Church, the mystical person of Christ, which is the presence of Jesus in our time. Through these gifts, our actions, then, will assist us in manifesting to others our belief in Jesus Christ. The gifts will help in making Him present to a world in need of His love.

THE ALBERT ARMSTRONG

The Twelve Fruits of the Holy Spirit

Read Luke 6:43–45 or Matthew 7:17–20.

In these Scripture verses, Our Lord talked about trees bearing good fruit and that good fruit comes from good trees and not bad trees. He said that just as we can know if a tree is good or bad by the fruit it bears, so a person (a prophet, in Matthew's Gospel) is known by his good works.

The gift of the Holy Spirit in Confirmation produces good qualities in the life of everyone who cooperates with the graces of the sacrament. These qualities are called the twelve fruits of the Holy Spirit, and they are signs that the Holy Spirit is operating in a person's life. Some of these gifts are mentioned in St. Paul's Letter to the Galatians, 5:22–23.

The twelve fruits of the Holy Spirit are the following:

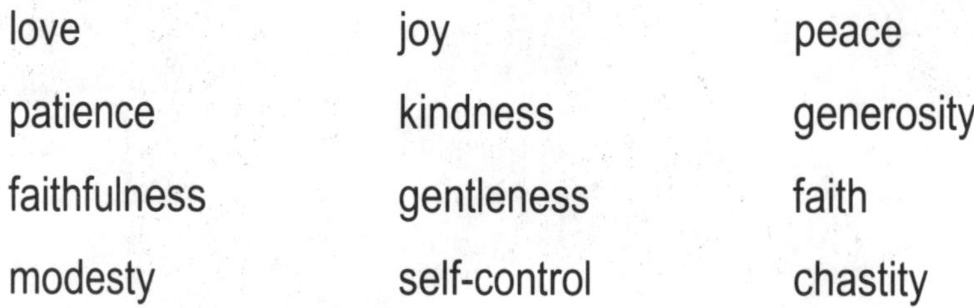

love	joy	peace
patience	kindness	generosity
faithfulness	gentleness	faith
modesty	self-control	chastity

When another person sees these qualities at work in a Christian's life, that person is seeing an indication that the Holy Spirit is at work.

RESPONDING TO THE HOLY SPIRIT

The same Holy Spirit Who is given to us in Confirmation in a special manner is active in many other ways. His work is to draw all persons to Jesus Christ and thus to the Church. We have learned that we should respond to the gift of the Holy Spirit in Confirmation, but it is important that we respond to the work of the Holy Spirit manifested in a variety of other ways.

In this chapter we will consider some of these other ways and how the graces given in Baptism and Confirmation help us to respond to these other manifestations of the Holy Spirit.

The Holy Spirit Moves Our Hearts in Prayer

The Holy Spirit prompts us to pray. As Catholics who have received the sacraments of Baptism and Confirmation, we should be responsive to His promptings.

How do we pray well? How do we know when we are being called to pray?

• To pray is to lift one's mind and heart to God. Prayer is a conversation with God. This means that during prayer we should be thinking about God and listening to His word, which will lead us to acts of love, praise, thanksgiving, petition, or repentance and may also lead us to make resolutions.

• Many times, when little children pray, they use formal prayers taught to them by their parents. These prayers can be very helpful in turning their minds and hearts to God. The words they use in their prayers have been provided by God and the Church. Examples of such prayers are the "Our Father", the "Hail Mary", the "Glory Be to the Father", the "Act of Contrition", and the Acts of Faith, Hope, and Charity.

• Some families and young people pray the Rosary, which is a combination of formal prayers with meditation (thinking) about important events in the lives of Jesus and Mary. We call these events "mysteries". In the Rosary, the Holy Spirit helps us to ponder special events in the lives of Jesus and His Mother. We can listen and learn from these events, as a way to love God and our neighbor more.

• Another form of prayer is quiet meditation, in which we listen to God the Holy Spirit, as He speaks to us in our minds. This does not mean that we hear inner voices talking to us, but it does mean that, through His grace, our minds are enlightened to understand and penetrate more deeply the message He has revealed through Jesus and the Church. By meditating, we follow the example of Mary, of whom the Scriptures say: "And Mary kept all these things, reflecting on them in her heart" (Lk 2:19).

• In quiet prayer, we may also see how a teaching of Jesus applies directly to a situation in our lives. Even if one does not have an enlightening thought, prayer will lead to a deeper love of God, the ultimate goal of all prayers.

A number of Catholic saints have developed different methods of meditative prayer. We will propose one method here.

◆

To use this method effectively, set aside approximately ten to fifteen minutes in a quiet place, every day if possible. The following steps can be used to pray:

1. Think about how God is present with you, because He has shared His life with you in Baptism. You may not be able to see or feel Him, but you know through faith that He is present.

2. Ask God to bless this time that you are able to spend with Him.

3. Take a short passage from Scripture or a devotional book and read it slowly. Or take a prayer, such as the "Our Father", and think about the words and their meaning.

4. Think about this passage or prayer and let God speak to you by enlightening your mind so that you will be able to understand it better or to apply it to your life in a new way.

5. Make an act of love for God based on your meditation. This act of love may include an act of resolution to do something good in your life or an act of repentance to change your behavior.

6. Close your prayer by thanking God for the opportunity to be able to spend time with Him in prayer.

◆

By using this type of meditative prayer we will deepen our love for God and our neighbor through the work of the Holy Spirit. We will become more like Jesus and thus be a better witness to our Faith.

To become more like Jesus is also the purpose of the gift of the Holy Spirit in Confirmation. So, by following these promptings of the Holy Spirit in prayer, we will be able to respond more fully to the graces of the sacrament of Confirmation, which assist us in spreading and defending the Faith by what we say and do.

The Holy Spirit Teaches Us in the Church

The same Holy Spirit Who speaks to us in prayer is the same Holy Spirit Who guides the Church when it is teaching us through the Pope and the bishops. The bishops are the successors of the Apostles. The Pope is the successor to the Apostle Peter. We can trace bishops back to the time of the Apostles, and we can trace the Popes back to St. Peter.

St. Peter and the other Apostles were given authority from Jesus to teach and guide the Church He founded. They received the gift of the Holy Spirit at Pentecost to guide them in their official teaching. Through the power of the Holy Spirit they teach in the name of Jesus Christ. That is why we can say that, when the Pope and the bishops together teach on Faith and morals, it is Jesus Who teaches. As we learned in Chapter 1, St. Paul came to the Church in Jerusalem to settle a dispute about whether or not the Gentiles had to be circumcised before they could be baptized. He met with St. Peter and the other Apostles, and they settled this dispute in the name of Jesus.

Because the Holy Spirit guides the official teachers of the Church, we know that they must be listened to and followed. To follow them is to follow Jesus. We have that guarantee. In fact, if we think that the Holy Spirit is telling us in prayer something that is contrary to what the Church teaches, we must always follow the Church. God is pure Truth, and He cannot contradict Himself. The Holy Spirit cannot say one thing to us through the Catholic Church and say the opposite to us in prayer. This is an impossibility.

What we may be hearing in prayer could be our emotions, our selfish desires, or a temptation from the devil. Therefore, we should always follow what we know to be God speaking to us—the official teachings of the Pope and the bishops.

When we follow the Pope and the bishops, who are guided by the Holy Spirit, we can be confident that we will become the good examples of the Faith to which we are called by our Baptism and Confirmation. We will be ambassadors of Jesus spreading and defending the Faith by what we say and do.

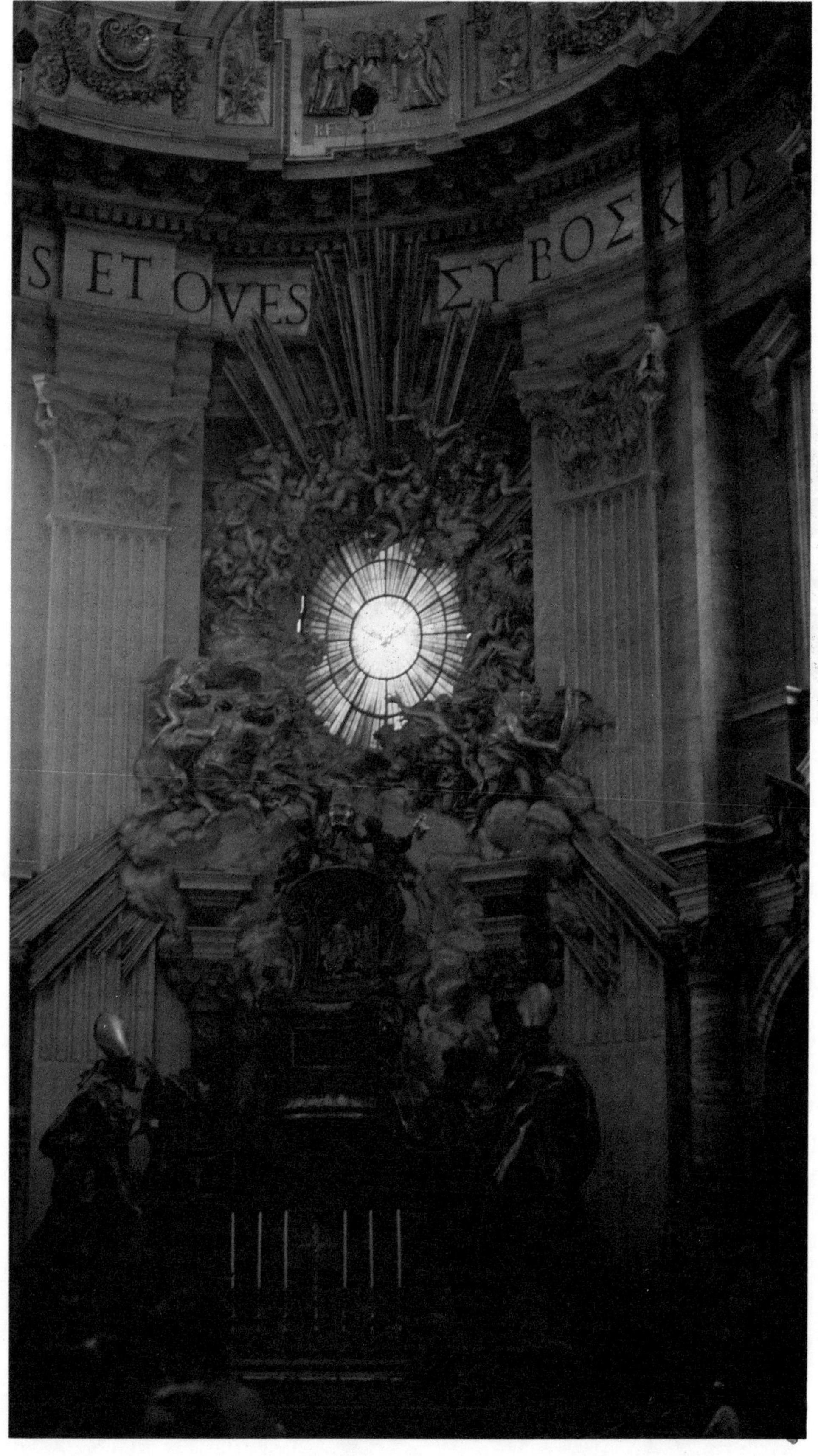

. . . if we think that the Holy Spirit is telling us in prayer something that is contrary to what the Church teaches, we must always follow the Church.

By the Power of the Holy Spirit We Have the Eucharist

In a beautiful stained-glass window above the main altar in St. Peter's Basilica in Rome one can see a picture of a dove. If fact, many Catholic Churches throughout the world have representations of a dove over the altar of the Eucharistic Sacrifice. The dove symbolizes the Holy Spirit, by Whose power the bread and wine become the Body and Blood of Jesus.

When a priest celebrates the Eucharist using Eucharistic Prayer III, he prays the following words over the bread and wine before the Consecration: "And so, Father, we bring you these gifts. We ask you to make them holy by the power of your Spirit, that they may become the body and blood of your Son, our Lord Jesus Christ, at whose command we celebrate this eucharist."

It is the Holy Spirit Who makes us holy through the sacraments. Through the work of the Holy Spirit, the sacraments give us grace, which Jesus merited by His death on the Cross and rising from the grave. When we worthily celebrate the sacraments, particularly the Eucharist, we receive grace and become holy—we become more like God.

It is the same Holy Spirit, Whom you will receive in the sacrament of Confirmation, Who is active in the Eucharistic liturgy. The Holy Spirit has complementary goals in these two sacraments.

In Confirmation, the Holy Spirit gives us the power and grace to spread and defend the Faith by what we say and do. This enables us to witness to Jesus, so that the whole world will come to know Him.

In the Eucharist, the Holy Spirit unites us to Jesus. We are united to His sacrifice on the Cross, we are united to Him when we receive His Body and Blood, and we are united to Him when we adore Him in the Blessed Sacrament. So, Confirmation and the Eucharist complement one another. Confirmation enables us to witness to Jesus, and the Eucharist unites us with Him.

Sin Keeps Us from Being Witnesses to Jesus and Deafens Our Ears to the Promptings of the Holy Spirit

The Holy Spirit guides us in the truth, so that we can love God with our all hearts and our neighbors as ourselves. Not only does He guide us in the truth, but He also calls us to do God's will in the day-to-day events of our lives. By listening to the gentle promptings of the Holy Spirit, particularly in prayer, we are able to know what God wants us to do to serve Him.

Just as a jet roaring over our homes can drown out the sound of someone talking to us, so, too, God's voice can be blocked out through sin. Sin can deafen us spiritually to the point that it becomes difficult or impossible to hear what the Holy Spirit is calling us to do.

If some persons are preoccupied with doing evil, abusing drugs, for example, they will be unable to focus their attention on God. They will be concerned about how they can get enough money to buy drugs or about the effects of these harmful chemicals. It will be almost impossible for these people to think of much more than themselves.

If someone has seriously offended another through an uncharitable deed, that individual needs to make peace with the person who was offended. A fractured relationship can be a major distraction for someone desiring to perceive God's will in prayer. Until peace with the offended person is achieved it will be difficult to make God the focus of spiritual growth. "Therefore, if you bring your gift to the altar, and there recall that your brother has anything against you, leave your gift there at the altar, go first and be reconciled with your brother, and then come and offer your gift" (Mt 5:23–24).

Even lesser sins (venial) can hinder growth in God's love. These offenses get in the way of our listening to the Holy Spirit's promptings.

It is important, then, for baptized and confirmed Catholics to take advantage of the sacrament of Reconciliation in order to turn away from sin and listen more attentively to the Holy Spirit. Not only does God forgive our sins in this sacrament, but He gives the grace to help us not to sin again. It is the work of the Holy Spirit in this sacrament of forgiveness that frees us from sin and the habit of sin. He moves our hearts to repentance, He gives the sacramental grace necessary for the forgiveness of our sins, and He bestows the strength not to sin again.

Of course, sin also hinders us from being a witness to Christ and His Church. Sin is a wrong choice. When we sin, we offend God, ourselves, and others. Rather than serving God and spreading the Faith by our actions, we act contrary to God and our Faith, and we are not proper witnesses to Christ.

The Holy Spirit gives us the grace to spread and defend the Faith by what we say and do. By frequently receiving the sacrament of Reconciliation, through which the Holy Spirit operates, we can conform our lives to that of Jesus. Thereby we become better witnesses to Jesus and accomplish the goal of the Holy Spirit—to bring all people to Jesus Christ.

The Holy Spirit Prompts Us to Respond to the Poor

He [Christ] is present in the Sacrifice of the Mass not only in the person of his minister, "the same now offering, through the ministry of priests, who formerly offered himself on the cross," but especially in the eucharistic species. By his power he is present in the sacraments so that when anybody baptizes it is really Christ himself who baptizes. He is present in his word since it is he himself who speaks when the holy scriptures are read in the Church. Lastly, he is present when the Church prays and sings, for he has promised "where two or three are gathered together in my name there am I in the midst of them" (Mt 18:20) .

Vatican Council II, *Constitution on the Sacred Liturgy*, no. 7

The work of the Holy Spirit is to lead us to Jesus Christ, Who is present to us in four ways in the Eucharist. He is present under the appearances of bread and wine (His most important presence), in the priest who celebrates the Eucharist, in the Word of God as it is proclaimed, and when two or three are gathered in His name. He is present also in the other sacraments.

Christ is also present to us in the poor. He identifies Himself in a special way with the poor, so much so that we show our love to Jesus when we help those who are poor.

To understand this, it is helpful to remember that Jesus became poor for our sake, particularly by dying on the Cross, because He gave everything to God the Father, including His life for our sake. He identified Himself specifically with the poor, so much that He was able to say, "Whatever you did for one of these least brothers of mine, you did for me" (Mt 25:40).

Mother Teresa and her religious sisters are examples for us of people who see Christ in the poor. Mother Teresa said that the women who become sisters in her community "want to give God everything. They know very well that it's to Christ the hungry and Christ the naked and Christ the homeless that they are doing it. And this conviction and this love is what makes the giving a joy" (*Something Beautiful for God*, pp. 105–7).

It is not always easy to see Christ in the poor. Mother Teresa wrote, "When we look at the Tabernacle, we understand how much Jesus loves us today. Jesus still keeps close to us in the Bread of Life. If we recognize Him there, we would be able to recognize Him in the distressing disguise of those we work with and be able to restore them to their lost dignity as children of God—our Brothers and Sisters. What gives us the faith to be able to do this is receiving Jesus in the Bread of Life and spending time with Him in the Holy Eucharist, in silent prayer and in praying the Rosary" (letter to Abbot McCaffrey, Fr. John Hardon, and members of Eternal Life Community, February 18, 1991).

The Holy Spirit draws us to Jesus, so our loving response to Him in the poor is initiated by the grace of the Spirit. This loving response will help us to fulfill our responsibilities to the graces of both our Baptism and our Confirmation. It is the same Holy Spirit working in a variety of ways to accomplish the one goal of drawing all people to Jesus.

Nevertheless the liturgy is the summit toward which the activity of the Church is directed; it is also the fount from which all her power flows. For the goal of apostolic endeavor is that all who are made sons of God by faith and baptism should come together to praise God in the midst of his Church, to take part in the Sacrifice and to eat the Lord's Supper .

Vatican Council II, *Constitution on the Sacred Liturgy*, no. 10

8 THE RITE OF CONFIRMATION

The sacrament of Confirmation confers the gift of the Holy Spirit. How does this happen? What actually takes place when you receive the sacrament?

As with most sacraments, there is simplicity and beauty connected with the action and words of the rite. Before the sacrament of Confirmation is administered, the bishop, who is the usual minister of Confirmation, extends his hands over the candidates and prays that the Holy Spirit will descend upon them. Then the bishop places his hand on the head of each candidate and with his thumb anoints the candidate's forehead with holy chrism. While he anoints the forehead, the bishop says the following words, "[Name of candidate], be sealed with the Gift of the Holy Spirit." The candidate responds "Amen."

This is the essence of the sacrament. The words tell what is taking place by the action of minister of the sacrament, namely, the pouring out of the Holy Spirit.

After he has confirmed a person, the bishop says, "Peace be with you." And the newly-confirmed responds, "And also with you."

The sacrament of Confirmation is usually administered during Mass, and it is preceded by the renewal of baptismal vows, so that those who are present will see the connection between the sacraments of initiation—Baptism, Confirmation, and the Eucharist. During the renewal of the baptismal vows, the candidates renounce sin and the temptations of the devil. In other words, the candidates express a desire to turn away from sin in their lives. The candidates also make a Profession of Faith, proclaiming their belief in all that the Catholic Church teaches.

The candidate is presented to the bishop by a sponsor, who "is to take care that the person confirmed behaves as a true witness of Christ and faithfully fulfills the duties inherent in this sacrament" (Code of Canon Law, canon 892). You are encouraged to choose a baptismal godparent as a Confirmation sponsor, so that the relationship between Baptism and Confirmation is highlighted. The sponsor must be at least sixteen years of age, a practicing Catholic who will help you fulfill the responsibilities of Confirmation, and someone who has already received the sacraments of Baptism, Confirmation, and the Eucharist. The sponsor cannot be a parent of the candidate.

You are encouraged to use your baptismal name in Confirmation, but another saint's name may be chosen to honor that saint and to make that saint your special patron.

Confirmation is the Pentecost event for every Catholic. The Holy Spirit is given so that you will be united more closely to Christ and the Church for the purpose of spreading and defending the Faith by word and deed.

ASSIGNMENTS

1.
An Interview with the Bishop Who Will Confirm You

CONFIRMATION AND SETTING GOALS

The sacrament of Confirmation is given to us to unite us more closely to the Church and to help us to spread and defend the Faith by what we say and do. Consequently, this sacrament should affect how we set our goals in life and how we meet those goals. As we set our goals with regard to spiritual life, vocation, education, occupation, friends, and entertainment, our Faith should be the most important consideration. Likewise, as we strive to meet these goals, our Faith should be the most important consideration. As members of the Church, we should be looking for ways in which to bring Christ to the world and to spread and defend the Faith in every area of daily living.

The usual minister of the sacrament of Confirmation is a bishop, because bishops are successors of the Apostles. The Apostles were present at the first Pentecost, when the Holy Spirit descended upon the Church. Because the sacrament of Confirmation is the Pentecost event for each Catholic, we can more easily see the connection between Confirmation and Pentecost if a bishop is the one who administers this sacrament. (In special situations, the bishop may give a priest the permission to administer this sacrament.)

Interview the bishop who will be administering the sacrament of Confirmation for your class and write a feature article based on your interview. You may want to ask the bishop some of the following questions:

1. Where did you grow up? How many brothers and sisters did you have?
2. How old were you when you entered the seminary? Before you entered the seminary, what kind of work did you do?
3. When did you become a priest? What influenced you to become a priest?
4. When did you become a bishop? How old were you when you became a bishop?
5. What kinds of work do you do as a bishop? What are your most important responsibilities?
6. In how many parishes do you administer the sacrament of Confirmation each year?
7. What is some important advice you would like to give young people to help them to prepare for the sacrament of Confirmation?
8. What concerns you most about young people?
9. Do you see opportunities for young people and adults to be courageous in witnessing to Christ and His Church?
10. What advice do you have for young people who are trying to discern the vocation to which God is calling them?

ASSIGNMENTS

2.
A Newspaper Article on Your Confirmation

In Chapter 1 you read a news account of Pentecost, when the Holy Spirit came upon Mary, the Apostles and the other followers of Jesus in the Upper Room. The reception of the sacrament of Confirmation will be the Pentecost experience for you.

Write a short news story giving the details of your Confirmation. You will want to make sure the journalist's six questions are answered in your article.

Include a brief explanation of the sacrament of Confirmation. Explain the essential elements of the rite in a way that even a non-believer can understand the event. Include some background about the bishop who will confirm you.

3.
How Will the Sacrament of Confirmation Affect Me?

The sacrament of Confirmation has a number of effects. These can have a positive impact upon the lives we live.

For instance, the sacrament deepens the seven gifts of the Holy Spirit. One of these gifts is fortitude. With the help of this gift you can overcome fear and speak courageously about the Catholic Faith.

Write at least a one-page paper on the effects of Confirmation, and how this sacrament will make a difference in the way you live your life as a Catholic. Keep this paper and after your Confirmation refer to it periodically as a reminder of what this sacrament has done in your life.

POPE JOHN PAUL II SPEAKS TO AMERICAN YOUTHS

On September 12, 1987, Pope John Paul II spoke in New Orleans to thousands of young people. He said:

"Prayer also helps us to be open to the Holy Spirit, the Spirit of truth and love, the Spirit who was given to the Church so that she could fulfill her mission in the world. It is the Holy Spirit who gives us the strength to resist evil and do good, to do our part in building up the kingdom of God.

"It is significant that the symbol of the Holy Spirit on Pentecost was tongues of fire. In fact, fire is often the symbol that the Bible uses to speak of the action of God in our lives. For the Holy Spirit truly inflames our hearts, engendering in them enthusiasm for the works of God. And when we pray, the Holy Spirit stirs up within us love of God and love of our neighbor."

SUGGESTED READINGS

Butler's Lives of the Saints (various editions).

The New American Bible with Revised New Testament (Washington, D.C.: Confraternity of Christian Doctrine, 1986).

Saint of the Day, ed. Leonard Foley, O.F.M. (St. Anthony Messenger Press, 1975).

Salon, Luke, *The Work Is Yours: The Life of St. John Baptist de la Salle* (Christian Brothers Publications, 1989).